95
93
94
126
72
74
77
76
78
80
81
82
85
124
127
142
136
148
150
151
101
98
100
88
96
109
112
128
140
90
91
86
92
108
110
114
115
117
116
118
120
122
141
144
123
130
132
131
102
104
106
134
138
84
152
146
154
156
158

WONDERS
OF THE
WORLD

WONDERS OF THE WORLD

100 incredible and inspiring places on earth

MARK TRUMAN

igloo

Published in 2007
by Igloo Books Ltd
Cottage Farm
Sywell
NN6 0BJ
www.igloo-books.com

10 9 8 7 6 5 4 3 2 1

ISBN: 978-1-84561-701-1

Designed by
THE BRIDGEWATER BOOK COMPANY

Printed in China

Contents

Moai Statues 8
Golden Gate Bridge 10
Yosemite National Park 11
Hoover Dam 12
Banff National Park 14
Grand Canyon 16
Yellowstone National Park 18
Barringer Meteorite Crater 19
Carlsbad Caverns 20
Mount Rushmore 21
Teotihuácan 22
Galapagos Islands 24
The Gateway Arch 26
Temples of Tikal 28
Chichén Itzá 30
Panama Canal 32
CN Tower 34
Niagara Falls 35
Statue of Liberty 36
Empire State Building 38
Machu Picchu 39
Amazon Rainforest 40
Iguazu Falls 41
Rio de Janeiro Harbor 42
Mezquita of Córdoba 43
Alhambra 44
Sahara Desert 46
Mont St. Michel 48
Stonehenge 50
Chartres Cathedral 52
The Channel Tunnel 53
Château de Chambord 54
Versailles 56
Eiffel Tower 58
Louvre Museum 60

Millau Viaduct 62
Fjords of Norway 64
Matterhorn 66
Marrakesh 68
Leaning Tower of Pisa 70
Neuschwanstein Castle 71
Canals of Venice 72
St. Mark's Basilica &
   Campanile 75
St. Peter's Basilica 76
Sistine Chapel 77
The Colosseum 78
Pompeii 80
Delphi 81
The Parthenon & the Acropolis 82
Victoria Falls 84
Hagia Sophia 85
Abu Simbel 86
Pyramids of Giza 88
Karnak Temple 90
Valley of the Kings 91
The Aswan High Dam 92
St Basil's Cathedral 93
Kremlin 94
Aurora Borealis 95
The Northern Red Sea 96
Jerusalem Old City 98
Petra 100
Baalbek 101
Serengeti Migration 102
Ngorongoro Crater 104
Mount Kilimanjaro 106
Mecca 108
Throne Hall of Persepolis 109
Burj Al Arab Hotel 110

Golden Temple 112
Amber Fort 114
Taj Mahal 115
Varanasi 116
Kathmandu Valley 117
Mount Everest 118
The Qinghai-Tibet Railroad 120
Potala Palace 122
Shwedagon Pagoda 123
Gobi Desert 124
Lake Baikal 126
The Great Wall of China 127
Lijiang 128
Temple of the Emerald
   Buddha 130
Petronas Twin Towers 131
Angkor Wat 132
Krakatoa Island 134
Qin Terracotta Warriors 136
Borobudur 138
Zhangjiajie National Forest
   Park 140
Hong Kong's Harbor
   & Cityscape 141
Forbidden City 142
Banaue Rice Terraces 144
Uluru/Ayers Rock 146
Akashi-Kaikyo Bridge 148
Temple of the Golden
   Pavilion 150
Mount Fuji 151
The Great Barrier Reef 152
Sydney Opera House 154
Milford Sound 156
Antartica 158

Picture Credits 160

Introduction

The world is bursting with a vast array of natural and fabricated wonders that provide us with a constant source of surprise, curiosity, and awe. In these pages we will learn about one hundred of those wonders, selected because they are superlative examples of nature's grandeur or outstanding human architectural and engineering achievements from prehistoric times to the present day. Our one hundred wonders are organized from west to east, starting from the International Date Line and continuing eastward across the globe. The maps found at the beginning and end of the book can be used as a guide along our route. Each wonder's approximate location is marked with its page number (though the sites do not always appear to be in correct west-to-east order on the maps as the Earth is, of course, round and our maps are not!). Prepare to be amazed!

NATURAL WONDERS

Nature is the creator of some of the planet's most wondrous locations and phenomena. From the stark beauty of the Sahara and Gobi deserts and the icescapes of Antarctica, to the verdant Amazon Rainforest, nature offers awe-inspiring extremes of landscape.

Nature has also produced outstanding individual features all over the planet, including:

† magnificent waterfalls, such as Victoria Falls in Africa and Niagara Falls in North America
† the fantastic fjords of Norway and Milford Sound in New Zealand
† beautiful bodies of inland water, such as Lake Baikal in Siberia
† spectacular underwater landscapes, such as those found in the Great Barrier Reef in Australia and the Red Sea in Egypt
† towering mountains, such as Kilimanjaro in Tanzania, the Matterhorn in Europe, and Mount Everest on the Tibetan-Nepalese border
† curious caves with amazing stalactites and stalagmites, such as those found in the Carlsbad Caverns in the USA
† breathtaking natural events, as evidenced by the volcanic eruptions of Krakatau in Indonesia in 1883 and Pompeii in Italy in 79 CE.

Some outstanding geographical features such as Mount Fuji in Japan and Uluru (Ayers Rock) in Australia are not just international icons but also have significant spiritual importance to indigenous peoples.

Nature is also the source of some wildlife wonders, such as the annual Serengeti migration of millions of wildebeest, zebra, and gazelles, and the Galapagos Islands, which teem with unusual creatures such as the Giant Tortoise and the Blue-footed Booby.

Often humans have sought to preserve areas of outstanding beauty, especially where wildlife is thriving, in national parks such as Yellowstone and Yosemite in the USA, Zhangjiajie in China, Banff in Canada, and—possibly the best place to view game in the world—the Ngorongoro Crater in Tanzania.

On the subject of natural wonders we should not forget nature's own fantastic firework display: the Aurora Borealis. The fact that there is a perfectly good scientific explanation for this phenomenon does not prevent the viewer from marveling at nature's wondrous magic.

RELIGIOUS WONDERS

Many of the world's architectural wonders have been inspired by the human desire to express spiritual awe and to honor gods. All of the current major religions have produced splendid edifices as a result of these desires. For example:

† Buddhism has produced the Temple of the Golden Pavilion in Kyoto, Japan; Shwedagon Pagoda in Myanmar; and the Temple of the Emerald Buddha in Bangkok, Thailand
† Christianity has produced Chartres Cathedral and Mont St. Michel in France; St. Basil's Cathedral in Moscow, Russia; and in Italy St. Peter's Basilica and the Sistine Chapel in Rome, St. Mark's Basilica and Campanile in Venice, and the Leaning Tower of Pisa
† Hinduism has produced Angkor Wat (subsequently reconsecrated as a Buddhist temple) in Cambodia
† Islam has produced the Al-Haram mosque in Mecca
† Hinduism has produced a plethora of temples in Varanasi in India
† Sikhism has produced the Harimandir Sahib, or Golden Temple, in Amritsar, India.

Some cities, such as Jerusalem Old City, bear witness to wonders from Christianity, Judaism, and Islam. Some buildings, such as the Mezquita in Córdoba in Spain and Hagia Sophia in Istanbul in Turkey, have been used as both mosques and Christian places of worship—an indication of their cities' mixed fortunes historically. Similarly, Kathmandu is the home to both Hindu and Buddhist temples and palaces that find their way onto this list of the world's top one hundred wonders.

WONDERS OF ANCIENT CIVILIZATIONS

Many ancient civilizations have left their architectural mark on the world in the form of wondrous buildings that provoke curiosity and debate about their origins and meaning. From the Stonehenge of prehistoric times to the buildings of the Ancient World, many surviving structural wonders give us clues to previous cultures, their religious rituals, and their ways of life. The Ancient Egyptians have bequeathed us the Pyramids of Giza, Karnak, and the Valley of the Kings; the Ancient Greeks the Parthenon and Delphi; the Ancient Romans the Colosseum and Pompeii; the Mayans Chichén Itzá and the Temples of Tikal; and the Incas Machu Picchu.

WONDERS OF MEDIEVAL AND EARLY MODERN ARCHITECTURE

Some of the world's most impressive buildings were erected purely as residences or memorials for royals and rulers. In France, the Château de Chambord, the Louvre, and Versailles were constructed at the behest of kings. Neuschwanstein Castle—our childhood fantasy medieval castle brought to life in Germany in the 1870s —was designed and commissioned by the mad King Ludwig of Bavaria. In India, the Taj Mahal was built by a grieving Mughal emperor as a mausoleum to his wife. Tibet's Potala Palace, China's Forbidden City, Spain's Alhambra Palace, and Russia's Kremlin are all architectural wonders built to house their country's great and good.

WONDERS OF MODERN ARCHITECTURE

Wonders of the modern world are often places of leisure or business, or structures that demonstrate the sheer ingenuity of state-of-the-art engineering skills. The Burj Al Arab Hotel in Dubai and the Sydney Opera House in Australia are examples of modern architectural wonders that inspire curiosity and admiration to such a degree that they elevate the structures to the status of international icons.

Superlatives such as "the highest" are applied to many modern edifices—at least at the time of their building, for they are constantly being superseded by ever higher structures. Still, some of the world's tallest include the skyscrapers of the Hong Kong skyline; the Empire State Building in New York; the Petronas Twin Towers in Kuala Lumpur, Malaysia; and the CN Tower in Canada (which is the world's tallest freestanding structure today).

WONDERS OF ENGINEERING

Modern history is awash with examples of our ever-growing engineering know-how. For example:

✝ canals, such as those of Panama and Venice, and undersea thoroughfares, such as the Channel Tunnel

✝ bridges, such as the Akashi Kaikyo Bridge in Japan, the Golden Gate Bridge in the USA, and the Millau Bridge in France

✝ railways, such as the Qinqhai Tibet Railway

✝ dams, such as the Aswan High Dam in Egypt or the Hoover Dam in the USA

✝ towers and monuments, such as the Gateway Arch and the Statue of Liberty in the USA, and the Eiffel Tower in France.

THE WONDER OF HUMAN WONDERS

The real human wonders are the ones that not only bear witness to the sheer ingenuity, creativity, and endurance of human activity (such as the Great Wall of China—the earth's longest construction—or the Banaue Rice Terraces in the Philippines), but that also express the exuberance and indefatigable nature of the human spirit. It is for that reason that this book includes not only wonders such as Stonehenge and the Alhambra, which inspire our curiosity and admiration, but also wonders such as Mount Rushmore and the marketplace of Marrakesh, which are testament to human achievement and the sheer *joie de vivre* that makes life itself the biggest wonder of all.

Moai Statues,
EASTER ISLAND

Nearly 1,000 striking stone statues ("moai") dominate the coastline of Easter Island, one of the most isolated spots in the South Pacific. Carved from volcanic rock and sometimes soaring up to 33 ft (10 m) high, the mysterious human figures have long provoked debate about their purpose and the lost culture that produced them.

Easter Island lies 2,250 miles (3,600 km) from the nearest inhabited land, Chile, which annexed it in 1888. The island was so named because the Dutch Admiral Jacob Roggeveen landed there on Easter Sunday in 1722. Today it is equally well known by its Tahitian name, Rapa Nui, the term also used for its language and inhabitants.

The people who carved the statues are believed to have been of Polynesian descent. Legend has it that they were led to the island by their king, Hotu Matua, who instigated a rich religious and artistic culture that included crafts such as tattooing, and wood and rock carvings.

The statues—mostly carved and erected between 1000 and 1650 CE—average 12 ft (4 m) in height and 14 tons in weight (as heavy as two very large elephants). They are thought to be symbols of political authority and power. They carry designs similar to islander tattoos indicating social position and some are topped by red stones, possibly symbolizing the red hair of the Rapa Nui elite. In addition to their political significance, ancient Polynesians believed that special carved objects were infused with a mystical spiritual force called *mana*, so it is likely that the statues were believed to be repositories of this force from their gods or chiefs.

Although often identified as "heads," the statues are actually heads and complete torsos. Some upright moai, however, have become buried up to their necks by shifting soils.

Golden Gate Bridge, USA

At the time of its completion in 1937, the Golden Gate Bridge in San Francisco, California, USA, was the longest of any suspension bridge in the world—spanning 4,200 ft (1,280 m). Now ranking seventh longest, it has nonetheless come to be an icon of San Francisco.

A San Francisco bridge project was initially envisioned by engineer Joseph Strauss in 1921 as a means for vehicles and pedestrians to cross the Golden Gate Strait, formerly possible only by ferry. Of many experts involved in the project, architect Irving Morrow played a major role, particularly in the selection of its Art Deco features and the distinctive orange-vermilion color, chosen to harmonize with natural features but also to stand out in fog which regularly builds up along the northern California coast.

Construction began in 1933 and the bridge was finally completed in 1937 at a cost of US$ 36.7 million; to rebuild it today would cost about US$ 1.2 billion.

Since its opening, some 1,800 million vehicles have traversed it, and currently about 100,000 vehicles cross the bridge via its six reversible lanes every day.

With its tremendous towers, sweeping main cables, and enormous span, the Golden Gate Bridge is acclaimed as one of the most beautiful bridges in the world.

...the distinctive orange-vermilion color, chosen to harmonize with natural features...

Yosemite National Park, USA

Renowned for its spectacular waterfalls and rock formations, Yosemite National Park in the Californian Sierra Nevada, USA, is also home to three groves of giant sequoia (Sierra redwood), the largest and one of the longest-living trees in the world.

Giant sequoia can live to be 3,000 years old and achieve heights of between 225 and 270 ft (75 and 90 m)—twice the height of the Statue of Liberty without the base. They can grow up to 33 ft (11 m) in diameter, as evidenced by the Wawona Tunnel Tree in the Mariposa Grove, the largest of Yosemite's sequoia groves. In 1881 a tunnel was cut through the tree and over the next 88 years stagecoaches and cars were driven through the opening until the tree toppled in 1969.

Other stars of Mariposa Grove include the Grizzly Giant, which, at about 2,700 years of age, is believed to be the oldest sequoia in existence, and the California Tunnel Tree, which has had people walking through its base since 1895. In all, the Mariposa Grove comprises about 500 sequoia, and these towering giants attract over three million visitors every year.

In spite of its size, the giant sequoia has a very shallow root system, but the roots can spread laterally over 225 ft (75 m).

At about 2,700 years old, the Grizzly Giant is believed to be the oldest sequoia in existence.

Hoover Dam, USA

The highest dam in the USA when it was completed in 1936 at a cost of US$ 165 million, the colossal Hoover Dam on the Arizona–Nevada border now ranks second-highest in the USA and eighteenth highest in the world.

One of the world's great feats of ingenuity and engineering, the Hoover Dam supplies 1.3 million people with hydroelectric power at a rate of four billion kilowatt-hours a year. The amount of water passing through the generators every second is the equivalent of over half the contents of an Olympic-sized swimming pool.

Work began on the 726-ft-high (242-m-high) dam in the Black Canyon area in 1931. Initially the river was redirected through huge tunnels created in the canyon walls, then 8,000 workers started to build the dam itself—which took five years.

The damming of the Colorado River created the reservoir of Lake Mead, named for Elmore Mead, the Bureau of Reclamation Commissioner at the time. At 115 miles (185 km) in length and between 1 and 10 miles (1.6 and 16 km) in width, Lake Mead is the biggest artificially created body of water in the USA.

Increasing numbers of visitors to the new reservoir led to the establishment of the Lake Mead Recreation Area in 1947, which today receives millions of swimmers, hikers, water-sports enthusiasts, and sightseers every year.

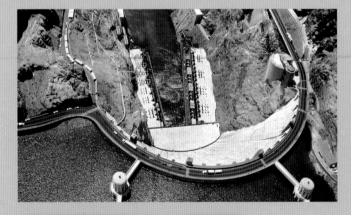

The Hoover Dam is a curved gravity dam. Lake Mead pushes against the dam, creating compressive forces that travel along the great curved wall. The canyon walls push back, counteracting these forces, making the dam very rigid.

Banff National Park,
CANADA

Home to grizlies, wolves, elks, and coyotes, Banff National Park in the Canadian Rocky Mountains offers some of the world's most impressive scenery, including glaciers, ice fields, dense forests, hot springs, and lakes.

The park's origins date from the discovery by railway workers of a cave containing hot springs in the mountains in Alberta in 1883. This led to a small area around the caves being deemed a protected reserve by Prime Minister John A. Macdonald in 1885. Originally named the Rocky Mountains Park, this was Canada's first national park.

Roads and railroad connections as well as the construction of two hotels near the hot springs and on Lake Louise resulted in the development of tourism in the area. Winter tourism was initiated with the Banff Winter Carnival in 1917, the highlight of which was a huge ice palace. The carnival popularized ski jumping, snowshoeing, and cross-country skiing.

Subsequently the park was expanded to its current size of 2,564 square miles (6,666 km²)—over five times the area of New York City—and renamed Banff National Park. Today the park receives about five million visitors throughout the year.

Sweeping vistas, glistening glaciers, and snow-capped peaks are all part of the allure of Banff National Park, nestled in the heart of the Canadian Rockies.

Grand Canyon, USA

One of the largest gorges in the world, the Grand Canyon in Arizona, USA, offers an awe-inspiring panorama and a vast interactive landscape that attracts over five million visitors annually.

The Colorado River is responsible for carving the canyon over many millions of years: the result is a gorge that measures 278 miles (446 km) long, between 0.3 and 18 miles (0.5 and 29 km) wide, and up to a mile (1.6 km) deep. The layers of sedimentary rock exposed by erosion—primarily water (and ice) but also wind—represent a significant record of geological time and are a major source of fossils. The oldest layer of rock containing fossils is bass limestone, which has existed for about 1,250 million years.

The site of several settlements of Native Americans, including the Navajo, for at least 4,000 years, the Grand Canyon first came to the attention of Europeans in 1540 when Spanish conquistador García López de Cárdenas led an expedition to explore the Colorado River.

The gorge has been part of the Grand Canyon National Park since 1991. The South Rim is the most accessible part of the canyon and is the scene of hiking, mule riding, river trips, and sightseeing flights by helicopter.

With its vast expanse and depth, the beauty of the Grand Canyon is breathtaking. There is an ever-changing panorama, from the first light of day until the sun sets on the distant horizon.

Yellowstone National Park, USA

Home to Old Faithful, probably the world's most famous geyser, Yellowstone National Park in Wyoming, Montana, and Idaho in the USA is officially the oldest national park in existence.

Established in 1872, the park ranges across nearly 3,500 square miles (about 9,000 km²)—the same area as Puerto Rico—on a high plateau surrounded by ranges of the Middle Rocky Mountains. Highlights of Yellowstone include its deep red Grand Canyon, nearly 20 miles (32 km) long, 1,000 ft (300 m) deep, and more than 2,500 ft (800 m) wide, embellished by over 40 waterfalls, including Lower, Upper, and Tower Falls. The waters of Lower Falls plunge about 300 ft (100 m), making these falls higher than Niagara Falls.

The park's geological features derive primarily from the various eruptions of the volcano directly beneath it. The last eruption some 640,000 years ago resulted in the Yellowstone Caldera, essentially a crater left by the exploding volcano, which measures 50 miles (80 km) long by 35 miles (55 km) wide and is one of the world's largest. Continuing volcanic activity means the park now boasts over 10,000 thermal features, including fumeroles (steam vents), mudpots (patches of mud where rising steam produces showers of mud), geysers, and hot springs.

Owing to its volcanic origins, the park contains nearly two-thirds of the world's geysers and hot springs, including Steamboat Geyser (the largest) and Old Faithful (the most regular). On average, Old Faithful erupts every 90 minutes, shooting up to 8,400 gallons (32,000 liters) of scalding water into the air. These eruptions can reach up to 180 ft (60 m) and may last for as long as five minutes at a time.

Yellowstone is also known for its fauna, and indeed is sometimes called the Serengeti of North America because of the vast array of magnificent wildlife roaming freely in its realms, including grizzly bears, black bears, bison, elk, moose, coyote, wolves, and pumas.

...the park contains nearly two-thirds of the world's geysers and hot springs...

Barringer Meteorite Crater, USA

The Barringer Meteorite Crater is a huge hollow created in the American Arizona Desert by the impact of a giant meteorite believed to have fallen to earth over 50,000 years ago. Although the meteorite itself was largely vaporized, its collision with the ground excavated 175 million tons of rock—the equivalent of a million of the world's largest whales.

The crater formed in the dry sandstone is over 1 mile (1.6 km) in diameter and 570 ft (190 m) deep, although the meteorite that created it measured only 150 ft (50 m) across. The crater rim comprises rocks (some as big as buildings) piled up to 150 ft (50 m) above the level of the land around the crater.

The meteorite was made of nickel-iron and weighed 300,000 tons. It hit the earth at a speed of about 28,600 miles (43,000 km) per hour. The force of the impact was some 150 times more powerful than the atomic bomb that devastated Hiroshima in World War II.

Although experts over the centuries have disputed the origin of the crater, mining engineer Daniel Moreau Barringer's 1902 theory of a meteorite impact has won the day. He showed that the crater contained millions of tons of powdery silica that could have been created only by the huge pressure of a meteoric impact and not by volcanic activity.

The crater was dubbed Barringer Crater in honor of Daniel Barringer, who was the first to suggest that it was produced by a meteorite impact.

The meteorite impacted the earth at a speed of about 28,600 miles (43,000 km) per hour.

Carlsbad Caverns, USA

One of over 300 colossal limestone caves dating back over 250 million years, the Carlsbad Caverns in the Chihuahuan Desert and Guadalupe Mountains of southern New Mexico and Texas, USA, are celebrated not only for their remarkable rock formations, such as Chinese Theater and Temple of the Sun, but also for the spectacular sight of thousands of bats leaving the caves at dusk.

Although there are indications of a Native American presence in the area as long as 12,000 years ago, and Spanish explorers are known to have visited the location during the 1500s, most credit for the discovery of the caves generally goes to a cowboy named Jim White, who first explored the caves in 1898.

Limestone caves are usually formed by water erosion in the guise of streams, but the Carlsbad Caverns were carved out of the rock by sulfuric acid. The result is a collection of awe-inspiring caves such as the Big Room and the Queen's Chamber, with spectacular stalagmite and stalactite formations, including Devil's Spring, Caveman, and Doll's Theater.

An exciting nightly natural phenomenon during the summer months is the exodus from the Carlsbad Caverns of about 4,000 Brazilian free-tail bats as they head off in search of food. Bats are known to have lived in the caves here for more than 5,000 years and during the early twentieth century their guano was mined for use as fertilizer. Today, however, interest is focused on the bats' flights to and from the caverns. Their homecomings following food trips are as spectacular as their departures. Just before dawn, they re-enter the caverns by diving from hundreds of feet In the air at speeds up to 25 miles (40 km) per hour.

...Carlsbad Caverns were carved out of the rock by sulfuric acid.

Mount Rushmore, USA

A remarkable American landmark recognized worldwide, the Mount Rushmore National Memorial in South Dakota, USA, is the name given to a monumental sculpture of presidential heads that attracts nearly three million visitors every year.

Carved from the granite 6,000 ft (2,000 m) up the mountainside in the Black Hills are, from left to right, the heads of former American presidents George Washington (1732–1799), Thomas Jefferson (1743–1826), Theodore Roosevelt (1858–1919), and Abraham Lincoln (1809–1865). Each head is nearly 60 ft (20 m) high and this impressive monument covers a surface area of about 2 square miles (5 km²).

The idea for the sculpture came from local historian Doane Robinson in 1923 with the aim of promoting tourism in South Dakota. He encouraged renowned sculptor Gutzon Borglum to investigate the project. Borglum selected Mount Rushmore, saying "America will march along that skyline." Borglum chose to feature Washington, Jefferson, Roosevelt, and Lincoln because they symbolized the first 150 years of American history and the spirit of the Republic.

Congress commissioned Borglum to begin the work in 1925. It took 400 workers about 14 years to complete the sculptures and cost nearly $US 1 million.

"America will march along that skyline."

Teotihuácan, MEXICO

At one time the biggest city in the Americas, Teotihuacán in Mexico dates from 200 BCE and is the enigmatic site of an ancient civilization that was once as powerful as the Roman Empire. Teotihuacán, meaning "city of the gods," is home to the Pyramid of the Sun, the third largest pyramid in the world.

Covering an area of over 11.5 square miles (30 km²) and supporting about 150,000 people, the ancient city of Teotihuacán features two particularly significant buildings along its Avenue of the Dead, the main thoroughfare of the city.

The stepped Pyramid of the Sun is the largest building on the site and one of the largest of its time in Mesoamerica. It measures 720 by 760 ft (240 by 254 m) and over 26 ft (72 m) high—about 1.5 times as high as the Statue of Liberty—and is thought to have been used for ritual activities associated with an unidentified deity.

The Temple of Quetzalcoatl (the feathered serpent deity) is situated in the Citadel in the Avenue of the Dead; it comprises a pyramid made from several platforms, and it features carved images of the feathered serpent. Evidence of human and animal sacrifice has been found at the site.

The sight of the ruins stretching along both sides of the extensive Avenue of the Dead shows how truly spectacular the city once was.

Galapagos Islands,
PACIFIC OCEAN

Teeming with strange and wonderful creatures, such as the Land Iguana, the Blue-footed Booby, and many others found nowhere else on earth, the Galapagos Archipelago presents an incomparable wildlife spectacle. Named for the Giant Tortoises found there, the archipelago comprises 13 main islands and six smaller ones about 600 miles (960 km) off the coast of Ecuador, South America.

A source of inspiration for Charles Darwin's *Origin of Species* (1859), the islands support a huge number of endemic species of flora and fauna, that is, species of plants, animals, and birds that are exclusive to these islands—and some of the species can only be found on one or two of the islands. It was this fact that led Charles Darwin, a young naturalist aboard the survey ship HMS *Beagle*, to develop his theory of evolution after a month-long visit to the islands in

1835. He discovered thirteen species of finches unique to the Galapagos Islands (now known as Darwin's finches) that led him to devise his theory of natural selection.

The isolated islands are home to an incredible array of birds and animals, including the Galapagos Penguin, sea lions, flamingos, and the Waved Albatross, as well as aquatic life such as the Sea Cucumber, harvested as a delicacy for top restaurants in Asia.

The iguana arrived on the Galapagos several million years ago from South America on floating vegetation. One group of iguanas took to the hills and the other to the sea.

The Gateway Arch, USA

At roughly half the height of the Empire State Building, the spectacular stainless steel structure known as the Gateway Arch soars to 630 ft (about 210 m) from the Mississippi riverside in St. Louis, Missouri, to assume the title of tallest monument in the USA.

The arch is the result of architect Eero Saarinen (1910–1961) winning a competition in 1947 to design the Jefferson National Expansion Memorial. The competition was a quest for a monument to honor the pioneering spirit of St. Louis, the "Gateway to the West," and to express the sense of liberty symbolized by Thomas Jefferson, the third president of the USA and author of the Declaration of Independence.

Construction of the arch began in 1963 and was completed in 1965 at a cost of US$13 million. Its scientific shape is called a catenary curve (the shape a chain takes when hanging freely between two supports). It can sway up to 18 inches (45 cm) in particularly windy conditions.

Trams take visitors to the top of the arch from where they can see up to 30 miles (50 km) beyond St. Louis and along the Mississippi River. The trams have carried over 25 million passengers since they began operation about 30 years ago.

A graceful monument to westward expansion in the USA, the arch's foundations have been sunk deep enough to help it withstand high winds and earthquakes.

Temples of Tikal,
GUATEMALA

Famed for its enormous Mesoamerican step-pyramid temples, Tikal ("Place of Voices") in Guatemala is one of the most important archeological sites of ancient Mayan civilization known to the world.

Construction of the monumental architecture at Tikal, in the tropical forests of the central Petén in Guatemala, started in the fourth century BCE, but its most fruitful period was between 200 and 850 CE when Tikal was an important Mayan political and cultural center. The six enormous step-pyramid temples, called Temples I–VI, were built over a 100-year period (approximately between 695 and 810 CE). One of the rulers of the period—Jasaw Chan K'awiil I (682–734 CE) is at rest in Temple I. Soaring up to 240 ft (77 m) high, Temple IV is the tallest of the six and was built in 741 CE.

The site, which in total covers about 23 square miles (60 km²), also contains the ruins of royal palaces, smaller pyramids, and stone monuments. It is believed the city was originally home to about 100,000 inhabitants.

Tikal was abandoned in the tenth century and was only brought to the attention of the outside world following a scientific expedition in 1848 by Modesto Méndez, Governor and Magistrate of the Petén region, and Ambrosio Tut, a gum-sapper. The city was declared part of Tikal National Park in 1955, the first of its kind in Central America.

Temple II, also known as the Temple of the Masks, stands at the western end of the Great Plaza and rises to a height of 120 ft (36 m). It faces Temple I across the plaza (see right).

Chichén Itzá, MEXICO

The ancient settlement of Chichén Itzá in the Yucatán Peninsula, Mexico, is the most important and vibrant known achievement of Mayan civilization still in existence. It is world-famous for El Castillo, the iconic pyramid temple that epitomizes the best of Mayan architecture.

Chichén Itzá developed here as nearby *cenotes* (sink holes) provided a vital source of water. Its name means "at the mouth of the wells of the Itzá people"—the Itzá being the Guatemalan Mayans.

A doorway at the base of El Castillo's northern stairway leads to a tunnel, from which you can climb steps to a room at the top of the interior temple, where King Kukulcán's Jaguar Throne is found.

The Mayans were highly advanced in the fields of architecture, art, astronomy, and writing, particularly in their Classic period (c. 250–900 CE), so it is no surprise that by 600 CE Chichén Itzá was a thriving city nor that, despite being mostly ruined, the city still has much to delight and amaze today.

The Temple of Kukulcán, also known as El Castillo ("The Castle"), is a stepped pyramid built between the 11th and 13th centuries CE. It was constructed on astronomical lines so that at the spring and fall equinox the rising and setting sun would cast the shadow of a huge writhing snake down the pyramid's steps.

Other architectural highlights of the city include the Templo de los Guerreros ("Temple of the Warriors"), named for its 200 columns—all carved to represent ancient Toltec combatants—and the Great Ballcourt, the largest known in ancient Mesoamerica. The Mayans were formidable sportsmen and the ballcourt was where teams met to play violent ball games often associated with ritual and sacrifice. One story has it that the captain of the winning team would offer his head for decapitation by the losers to turn him into a god, gaining him a direct route to heaven.

Panama Canal,
CENTRAL AMERICA

That the Panama Canal today rapidly transports about 14,000 vessels 50 miles (80 km) between the Pacific and Atlantic oceans is the legacy of a hard-won battle against geography, climate, and disease. Costing over 27,000 lives and US$ 375 million in its construction, the canal is nonetheless testament to human ingenuity and determination to triumph over adversity.

The shortcut between the two oceans that the waterway provides means ships can avoid sailing the treacherous seas around Cape Horn in the south of Chile and vastly reduce journey distance. For example, the 14,000-mile (22,500-km) voyage from New York to San Francisco is more than halved.

The canal was originally conceived of by Vasco Núñez de Balboa in 1513 when he discovered that only a narrow stretch of land separated the Pacific from the Atlantic. However, it was not until a French scheme was accepted in 1880 that attempts to build a canal began in earnest. This scheme for a sea-level canal was subsequently abandoned in 1893 owing to yellow fever, landslides, and poor equipment.

The USA under President William McKinley bought the project and began work on it in 1904. A revised version involving a locks system that raises ships up to 85 ft (28 m) above sea level was finally completed through the labor of over 56,000 people in 1914 CE, when it was inaugurated by the SS *Ancon*.

Workers battled against the difficulties provided by mountain ranges, jungles where the temperature often reached 90°F (30°C), floods, and landslides, as well as diseases such as malaria and yellow fever. The result is that today the canal is one of the world's most important shipping routes, employing about 9,000 workers and offering transit to commercial transportation activities that represent about five percent of world trade.

CN Tower, CANADA

A celebrated feature of Toronto's skyline, the CN Tower soars to over 1,815 ft (605 m)— that's not far short of two Eiffel Towers— bringing Canada the kudos of having the world's tallest freestanding structure.

Although it was designed to be an icon of the city, the tower also has a serious function as an important telecommunications hub. At the time when it was built, the growth of skyscrapers in the city had begun to cause communications interference. The tower's microwave receptors are at 1,109 ft (370 m) and its antenna is at 1,815 ft (605 m), with the result that Toronto's residents now experience excellent communications reception.

The skyline of Canada's largest city is defined by the CN Tower's great height and unique shape.

The tower was constructed in 1976 by Canadian National, the railroad company that gave the tower its name, as a symbol of the might of Canadian industry. The tower subsequently became a public company and passed into the hands of Canada Lands.

CN Tower has much to offer the two million visitors it receives annually, including a glass floor and outdoor observation deck at 1,122 ft (374 m), a cafe with panoramic views and, at 1,150 ft (383 m), a restaurant with a rotating floor that affords diners a 360-degree view of the city. The tower's major attraction, however, is the Sky Pod, the world's highest public observation deck, at 1,465 ft (488 m)—that's ten Statues of Liberty high!

...an icon of the city, the tower also has a serious function as an important telecommunications hub.

Niagara Falls, NORTH AMERICA

Astride the border of Canada and the USA near Toronto and Buffalo respectively, the immense Niagara Falls offer some of the most wondrous water cascades in the world—second in size only to Victoria Falls in southern Africa.

Niagara Falls in fact comprise three falls that occur either side of a mid-river obstacle in the form of Goat Island. On the eastern (American) side of the island are the American Falls and the much narrower Bridal Veil Falls. Neither of these, though, is as powerful or spectacular as the Horseshoe Falls that developed on the western (Canadian) side of the island.

The Horseshoe Falls, named for their shape, are about 2,600 ft (870 m) wide. About 90 percent of the nearly 202,000 cubic feet (5,700 cubic m) of water cascading over Niagara every second does so via these falls and it drops over 170 ft (57 m) in total. Tourism to the region has been growing since the 18th century and today the falls receive over 20 million visitors a year.

The Horseshoe Falls are also the subject of Native American legend. According to Iroquois lore, tribe members living by Niagara were mysteriously dying. Lelawala, the beautiful daughter of Chief Eagle Eye, was to be sacrificed to appease the Thunder God Hinum, who inhabited a cave behind the falls together with his two sons. She boarded a sacrificial canoe and plunged over the falls. However, she was saved by the two sons, and she promised herself to the brother who could reveal the secret behind the Iroquois deaths. One explained that a giant water snake was poisoning the water and eating the tribe members who died after drinking it. She told her tribe and they slaughtered the snake, which curled in a semicircle at the top of the waterfall thereby giving rise to its horseshoe shape. Lelawala is said to live in the cave behind the falls and to rule as Maid of the Mist.

Thrill-seekers have found fame at Niagara Falls in the past. Annie Edson Taylor went over the falls in a barrel at the age of 63 in 1901. She survived; others have not been so fortunate.

...today the falls receive over 20 million visitors a year.

Statue of Liberty, USA

Presented as a gift of the French people to mark the centennial of the Declaration of Independence, the Statue of Liberty is one of the USA's most widely recognized icons.

The Statue of Liberty was often one of the first glimpses of the USA for millions of immigrants after long ocean voyages from Europe.

French sculptor Frédéric Auguste Bartholdi designed the colossal copper statue, and is said to have modeled the face of the statue on his mother. The steel frame used to support the 151-ft-high (50-m-high) statue was created by Gustave Eiffel, the engineer responsible for the famous Parisian tower.

The statue was intended to be ready in 1876, in time for America's hundred-year celebration of its Declaration of Independence. However, political and funding problems meant that the statue did not arrive in the USA until 1886—ten years late. It now stands on Liberty Island in New York Harbor where it famously greets new arrivals and returnees to the country.

The statue features Lady Liberty. At her feet are smashed shackles, symbolizing freedom from oppression. She wears a crown with seven spikes that are said to indicate the world's seven seas and seven continents. In her raised hand she carries a torch, representing enlightenment; in the other hand she holds a tablet inscribed with the date of American Independence (July 4th 1776).

Empire State Building, USA

The 102-story Empire State Building in the USA offers one of the best vantage points for viewing New York's awe-inspiring skyline. When it was completed in 1931, it was the world's tallest building, a title it held for nearly forty years; today it ranks ninth in the world and second in the USA after the Sears Tower in Chicago.

Architect William Lamb based his design for the Art Deco building on the clean, straight lines of a pencil. Construction, which began in 1930, made use of innovatory building techniques such as the assembling of factory parts on site that helped to speed up the process. The building was completed in just over a year, taking seven million man hours and costing a total of about US$ 41 million.

The façade of the Empire State Building is composed of vast quantities of Indiana limestone and granite.

The construction of the tower, which soars to 1,453 ft (484 m), coincided with the Great Depression, which meant it did not break even renting out office space until 1950. However, in its first year it took US$1 million from visitors to its observatory on the 86th floor, which offers a 360-degree panoramic view of the Big Apple. On a clear day it is possible to see over 60 miles (100 km) to the countryside of Pennsylvania.

William Lamb based his design for the Art Deco building on the clean, straight lines of a pencil.

Machu Picchu, PERU

Often described as the Lost City of the Incas, the 15th-century city of Machu Picchu (meaning "manly peak") perches on a mountain top over 8,000 ft (2,500 m) up in the Peruvian Andes.

Developed between 1460 and 1470 under the eye of Incan ruler Pachacuti, Machu Picchu is believed to have functioned as a royal residence or religious retreat rather than as a trade or military center because of its remote, lofty location.

Its isolated site meant also that it escaped the notice of the invading Spanish conquistadors. Once home to about 1,200 people, its 200 buildings, including temples and houses surrounding communal courtyards, are remarkably well-preserved.

Significant highlights of the city were all constructed to honor the Incan sun god, Inti.

Among them are the Room of the Three Windows and the Intihuatan—a form of sun dial on which the Incas would "tie the sun to the post" at the winter solstice to ensure it would never leave them.

Crops grown at Machu Picchu included maize and potatoes, and the Incans used highly sophisticated irrigation and terrace-farming techniques to maximize their harvest.

Machu Picchu fell out of favor after Peru was conquered by Spain in 1532. Hiram Bingham, an explorer and Professor of South American History at Yale University, is credited with rediscovering the lost city in 1911.

Machu Picchu is believed to have functioned as a royal residence or religious retreat...

Amazon Rainforest, SOUTH AMERICA

Covering over 2,300,000 square miles (6,000,000 km²) of South America, the Amazon Rainforest represents the largest area of tropical rainforest in existence. Over half of it is located in Brazil (with the rest distributed in Peru, Venezuela, Ecuador, and other countries of the Amazon Basin), and it is home to one of the richest arrays of plant and animal life on earth.

Often referred to as the "lungs of the planet" because it produces 20 percent of the world's oxygen, the Amazon Rainforest developed around the world's largest river. The Amazon begins in the Andes of Peru and meanders 3,969 miles (6,350 km) across South America until it meets the Atlantic Ocean, where its vast delta is home to about half of the entire species of flora and fauna in the world.

Over 500 types of mammal (including sloths, howler monkeys, and the nocturnal kinkajous), 400 reptile species (among them the tree frog), 30 percent of the world's birds (including monkey-eating harpy eagles), and an amazing 30 million types of insect (including leafcutter ants, millipedes, and scorpions) can be found in the hot, humid conditions of the rainforest. The average temperature in the Amazon Basin is 79°F (26°C) and the region receives about 80 in (200 cm) of rainfall a year, compared with about 23 in (58 cm) for London and 47 in (120 cm) for New York.

To date, over 20 percent of the rainforest—nearly 232,00 square miles (603,200 km²), an area bigger than Texas—has been devastated by logging activities and land clearance, and the destruction is continuing apace. If this rate of annihilation—which includes the estimated loss of 130 species of flora and fauna every day—continues at its current level, the whole of the rainforest could disappear within 40 years. However, increasing amounts of land are becoming conservation areas, which might help to slow the pace of deforestation in the future.

...referred to as 'the lungs of the planet' because it produces 20 percent of the world's oxygen...

Iguazu Falls, SOUTH AMERICA

The spectacular, roaring Iguazu Falls grace a 2.5-mile-wide (4-km-wide) rim on the border between Brazil and Argentina, and comprise over 270 individual waterfalls, with some cascades as high as 269 ft (90 m) (nearly as high as London's Big Ben).

Second only to southern Africa's Victoria Falls, Iguazu Falls were first brought to the attention of the world by the Spanish conquistador Alvar Nuñez Cabeza de Vaca (1490–1557), who led an expedition to the region in about 1540. A fall on the Argentinian part of the rim is named after him.

Probably the most striking of all the falls is the Garganta del Diablo ("Devil's Throat"), a 2,300-ft (770-m) semicircle of thundering waterfalls right on the border that provides the world's most powerful cascade.

The name "Iguazu" is believed to derive from *y* and *guasu*, which mean "big" and "water" respectively in Guarani, the language of the indigenous people. According to traditional folk tales, the great waterfalls were created by a god who tried to marry a beautiful human woman. When she spurned him and escaped by canoe with her human lover, the god produced waterfalls to thwart her escape.

Probably the most striking of all the falls is the Garganta del Diablo ('Devil's Throat')...

Rio de Janeiro Harbor, BRAZIL

The vibrant Brazilian city of Rio de Janeiro developed between lush mountains and Guanabara Bay on the Atlantic Ocean around one of the most spectacular natural harbors in the world. The harbor's setting includes the world-famous white sand beaches of Copacabana and Ipanema, the rocky outcrop Sugar Loaf Mountain, and Tijuca Forest, which is the largest urban wooded area in the world.

It is easy to see why Rio's inhabitants call it the *cidade maravilhosa* ("marvelous city"), not least because of the city's beach culture. Rio's 110 miles (176 km) of beaches are witness not only to sunbathing and swimming, but also to sports, socializing, and parties on a huge scale (about two million people attend the New Year party at Copacabana every year).

Towering 1,300 ft (430 m) above Rio is Sugar Loaf Mountain, named for its resemblance to a sugar loaf. (Brazil is one of the world's leading producers of sugar.) Sugar Loaf is one of several *morros* (rounded peaks) in the region. Its summit can be accessed by a two-stage cablecar, updated since its 1912 debut, one that offers a breathtaking journey between Sugar Loaf and the lower peak of Morro da Urca. Sugar

Loaf, Morro da Urca, and Morro da Babilonia make up one of the world's largest urban climbing areas.

Declared a National Park in 1961, Tijuca Forest is a mountainous rainforest that covers over 12 square miles (32 km^2). It is home to many endangered rainforest plants and animals, and accommodates the Christ the Redeemer statue on its Corcovado Mountain.

Legend has it that Portuguese explorers named the bay Rio de Janeiro (which translates as "River of January") because when they arrived there in January 1502 they believed it to be the mouth of a huge river rather than a bay. The city itself was not officially founded until the arrival of the Portuguese knight Estácio de Sá in 1565. Brazil gained its independence in 1822, and Rio de Janeiro served as the country's capital until 1960, when the title was transferred to the newly built Brasília. Today Rio de Janeiro is home to about six million people.

Christ the Redeemer, an Art Deco-style statue of Jesus Christ, stands at the peak of Corcovado Mountain, overlooking the city.

...Portuguese explorers named the bay Rio de Janeiro (which translates as 'river of January')...

Mezquita of Córdoba, SPAIN

The pride of Córdoba in Spain, the Mezquita was once the second largest mosque in the world at a time when Córdoba was one of the most prosperous cities in Europe, a leading light in science, art, and culture. However, the Mezquita has also functioned as a Catholic cathedral, and the result is an architecturally diverse building that symbolizes the mixed fortunes of the city.

Commissioned by Abd ar-Rahman I, the first Muslim Amir (ruler) of Córdoba, the mosque was begun in 784. The building was enhanced and added to until 987, at which time it was considered the most splendid of the city's 1,000 mosques.

The Mezquita incorporates giant arches, 850 striking columns constructed of jasper, granite, and marble, and highly decorated prayer alcoves. However, its most magnificent feature is the *mihrab* (prayer niche), an exquisite marble dome covered in gold Byzantine mosaics. At one time an original copy of the *Koran* and a bone from the Prophet Muhammed were kept here, turning the mosque into a major pilgrimage site. Traditionally, the *mihrab* in a mosque faces Mecca, but Mezquita's *mihrab* does not, which renders it unique among mosques.

Increasing the building's singularity further are certain Christian architectural features, including chapels and a 16th-century Baroque cathedral with an elaborately carved ceiling. These were added subsequent to King Ferdinand III taking Córdoba from the Moors in 1236 and ordering the reconsecration of the Mezquita as a Christian church.

The Mezquita is most notable for its striped brick and stone arches, as well as over 850 pillars of jasper, marble, and granite.

At one time an original copy of the *Koran* and a bone from the Prophet Muhammed were kept here...

Alhambra, SPAIN

Perched high on a hillside plateau overlooking Granada in southern Spain with views of the Sierra Nevada, the Alhambra is a splendid 14th-century Moorish palace best known for its ornate decor, serene courtyards, and enchanting water features.

Alhambra's name may be associated with the founding ruler of the Nasrid dynasty, Muhammed Ibn Al Ahmar, but it may also refer to the red bricks used for the outer walls (*alhambra* means red in Arabic) that give the building its appealing warm glow.

Constructed between 1238 and 1354 as a residence and citadel for the Muslim rulers of Granada, the intention was to create a representation of paradise on earth through the use of exquisite architecture and design. Almost every surface throughout the building has been lavishly decorated, often using arabesques (a complex, ornate pattern of flowers, leaves, and geometric designs).

The main complex comprises the royal palace, including the *mexuar* (administrative buildings), the *serallo* (a series of rooms and courtyards, including the striking Patio of Myrtles and the splendid Hall of the Ambassadors in the Comares Tower), as well as the harem, of which the spectacular Lions' Court is the center.

The Alhambra is a sprawling palace-citadel comprising royal residential quarters, court complexes, a bath, and a mosque.

One of Spain's most visited tourist attractions, the Lions' Court not only contains prime examples of arabesques, it is also the site of the Fountain of Lions, an alabaster basin supported by twelve figures of lions in white marble.

Sahara Desert,
NORTH AFRICA

The Sahara is the largest desert in the world outside the polar regions. It sweeps across North Africa from the Atlantic Ocean in the west to the Red Sea in the east, covering an area of about 3,500,000 square miles (9,100,000 km²). You could fit England into it 70 times or the USA, minus Texas, once.

Despite common perception, only about a quarter of the desert's landscape is made up of sand dunes: it mostly comprises stone plateaux, gravel plains, dry valleys, and salt flats.

At first sight, there would seem to be little here to promote human or animal life, particularly given the extremes of temperature (from 21°F [-6°C] at night soaring to 136°F [58°C] in some places during the day). However, about 2.5 million people (as well as large numbers of jackals, jerboas, horned vipers, and antelopes) are pleased to call it home.

Despite its harshness, the Sahara offers a number of oases and waterfalls at its borders as well as some of the most breathtaking scenery in the world.

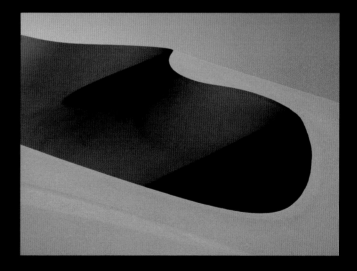

Over 25 percent of the Sahara's surface is covered by sand sheets and dunes—and draa, the mountainous sand ridges that dominate, can reach over 1,000 ft (333m).

Mont St. Michel,
FRANCE

The most-visited site in France after the Eiffel Tower and Versailles, Mont St. Michel is a magnificent tidal island that juts out of the sea off Normandy's northern coast, and presents its architectural splendor like a scene from a fairytale.

Tradition has it that the local bishop of Avranches, St. Aubert, was visited by the Archangel Michael in 708 and commanded to construct a church on the island. At first the bishop ignored the vision, but after a second visit by Michael a chapel was duly built, and it quickly became a popular pilgrimage site.

In the 11th century Italian architect Guillaume de Volpiano was commissioned to design the splendid Romanesque abbey church that dominates the summit of the island. Monastical buildings soon joined it and were further developed during the following century. When Philip II (1165–1223) prevailed in Normandy in the early 13th century, he gave Mont St. Michel a major financial boost that enabled it to develop the architectural splendor we see today. Subsequently the cathedral gained an extravagant Gothic chancel in the 15th century,

and it is crowned with a gold-leaf statue of St. Michael by French sculptor Emmanuel Frémiet (1824–1910).

The abbey was converted into a prison during the French Revolution in 1789, but in 1874 it was largely restored and became a national monument, thanks in part to the campaigning of Victor Hugo (author of *Les Misérables*).

At high tide the island is surrounded by sea; at low tide a half a mile (one-kilometer) stretch of sand joins it with the mainland. A causeway was added in 1879, but the sands (mostly fields of shifting quicksand) and the rapid turn of the tide have caught out many unsuspecting pilgrims. The dangers were shown in the Bayeux Tapestry (c. 1077), which features a visit to Mont St. Michel by William the Conqueror and Harold the Saxon.

Stonehenge, UK

Stonehenge is one of the most significant and intriguing prehistoric sites in the world. Located near Salisbury in Wiltshire, England, this mysterious circle of huge standing stones up to 22 ft (4.1 m) has provoked much speculation as to its purpose, including theories about astronomy and human sacrifice.

Stonehenge has undergone several stages of development: from a circular bank and ditch enclosure in about 3100 BCE to a timber structure, to the final stone version completed about 1500 BCE, the remains of which attract visitors from all over the world today. Its impressive construction includes bluestones, each weighing about four tons, which were transported on sledges and rollers over a distance of 150 miles (250 km) from the Preseli Hills in Wales—an extraordinary feat in its day.

Some experts believe Stonehenge had an astronomical function, acting as a form of prehistoric calendar for either religious or farming purposes. The stones are so aligned that at the summer solstice the sun shines directly through the center of the circle, and at the winter solstice a similar effect is seen at sunset. This theory ties in with sun worship practiced at the time, and with the idea of a farming calendar, since the arrival of the equinoxes marking the change in season would be significant for farmers.

Others believe that the site had a purely ritual purpose, serving as a place for cremated burials, and that Stonehenge acted as a temple in which humans could communicate with their gods and the spirits of their ancestors.

Whatever the truth about their purpose, the stones have inspired many folk stories. Geoffrey of Monmouth (1100–1155 CE), who popularized the tales of King Arthur, has it that the magician Merlin used his supernatural powers to transport the stone circle to Wiltshire from Ireland as a monument to 600 dead soldiers.

Chartres Cathedral, FRANCE

Deemed a masterpiece of Gothic architecture, the medieval Chartres Cathedral is celebrated for its fine carvings and stained glass, and is to be found about 50 miles (80 km) from Paris.

The current building was constructed between 1194 and 1220 on the site of an earlier Romanesque cathedral. The updated version, which now includes lofty aisles and soaring spires rising to over 300 ft (100 m) —one of which is among the world's top ten highest— continued to house a tunic (the *Sancta Camisia*) believed to belong to the Virgin Mary. It was presented to Chartres in 876 by Charles the Bald to celebrate his return from Jerusalem. The presence of this relic has meant that the cathedral has been a major Marian pilgrimage destination for hundreds of years.

The cathedral's nave is an immense 427 ft (142 m) long and 121 ft (40 m) high, with transepts to the north and south to conform to a cruciform plan. The lofty vaults are grounded by innovative flying buttresses, which not only support the height but also allow room for the magnificent stained-glass windows. The glasswork famously features a vibrant blue, particularly in a window showing Mary with the baby Jesus. Among more than 150 surviving pieces—together considered one of the finest collections of medieval glasswork in the world—is an astonishing highlight: the rose window, an intricate, circular window donated by the French Queen Blanche of Castile (1187–1251).

Stone carvings of sword-wielding soldiers and crosses are coupled with sculptures of Biblical scenes to create an opulent environment of high art that makes the cathedral one of the most spectacular in the world.

Chartres Cathedral marks the high point of French Gothic art. The vast nave, the porches adorned with fine sculptures, and the stained-glass windows combine to make it a masterpiece.

...the cathedral has been a major Marian pilgrimage destination for hundreds of years.

The Channel Tunnel, EUROPE

At just over 31 miles (50 km) long, the Channel Tunnel joining Folkestone, Kent, in England with Coquelles, Pas-de-Calais, in France is the longest undersea channel and the second longest rail tunnel on the planet.

Nearly two centuries in the planning, the Channel Tunnel was finally opened by Queen Elizabeth II and the then French President François Mitterrand in Calais in 1994. A tunnel link between England and France had first been suggested by French engineer Albert Mathieu-Favier in 1802 and would have taken the form of a thoroughfare for horse-drawn vehicles. Further proposals, including a floating steel tube, were subsequently made ,and tunneling was even initiated in 1922 and 1974 . However, it was only with the signing of the Franco-British Channel Fixed Link Treaty in 1986 that the project finally got underway.

Constructed at a depth of 150 ft (50 m) below the Channel seabed, the tunnel took over seven years and more than 15,000 workers to finish. The completed Channel Tunnel, which cost about £10 billion, actually comprises three parallel tunnels: two rail tunnels and a smaller service tunnel which gives access to the rail tunnels for regular maintenance or emergencies.

Today about eight million passengers travel through the tunnel every year on the high-speed rail link, Eurostar, and the tunnel's shuttle train service, Eurotunnel, carries over three million cars, trucks, and coaches annually. These figures are set to increase with the launch of the Channel Tunnel Rail Link to London—Britain's first new railroad in 60 years.

Today, trains roar through the tunnel at speeds of up to 100 miles (160 km) per hour. A journey through the tunnel takes about 20 minutes.

...the tunnel took over seven years and more than 15,000 workers to finish.

Château de Chambord, FRANCE

Chambord is the largest and most lavish castle in the Loire Valley, France. Commissioned by François I in 1519 as a hunting lodge, the chateau is a prime example of French Renaissance architecture, as it harmonizes medieval features with the symmetry and elegance espoused by the Renaissance.

The château, with its 440 rooms, 84 staircases, and 365 fireplaces, took 2,000 men about thirty years to construct. Typically medieval features, such as the central keep with its four huge towers, blend with Italian Renaissance concepts, as exemplified in its open galleries and roof terraces.

The original model for the château was devised by Italian architect Domenico da Cortona. However, it was the custom of François I to invite great minds in the arts and sciences to appear at court, including Leonardo da Vinci, and Da Vinci's general influence on the château's design is widely acknowledged. In particular, he is thought to have created the château's interlocking double-spiral staircase. This ingenious design—two adjacent flights of stairs that do not meet— supported by eight square pillars, forms the centerpiece at Chambord.

Château de Chambord is truly royal in its grandiose scale. It was built to serve only as a hunting lodge for King François I, and during his reign the castle was rarely inhabited.

The château narrowly escaped demolition following the French Revolution in 1789, but its furnishings were plundered at that time. Despite brief residency by its various owners, the château was abandoned for long periods and subsequently went into decline until it became the property of the state in 1930. A thirty-year restoration program began after World War II and today the castle is one of the biggest tourist attractions in France, receiving thousands of visitors annually.

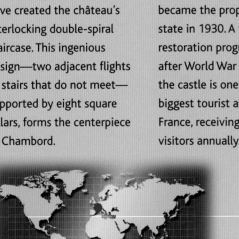

Versailles, FRANCE

Although it began life as a hunting lodge in the countryside not far from Paris, France, Versailles was to become one of the largest and most opulent palaces in the world.

Originally commissioned by Louis XIII in 1624, the building was added to by Louis XIV to such an extent that by 1682 the royal court (numbering thousands of people, including staff) had moved to Versailles. The palace became the seat of government for most of the period up to 1789, when Louis XVI was forced by the Revolutionaries to return to Paris before being sent to the guillotine in 1793.

Under Louis XIV Versailles gained one of its most famous features—the Hall of Mirrors. Measuring 220 ft (73 m) in length by 30 ft (10 m) wide and over 36 ft (12 m) high, the Hall contains 17 huge (and hence enormously expensive) arched mirrors on the wall facing the 17 windows onto the immense, ornate formal gardens. The room's decoration is exquisite and includes 24 gilded candelabra as well as some of Louis XIV's grandest statues and Roman emperor busts.

Its ceiling is painted with scenes of Louis in triumphant form, including one of him dressed as a Roman emperor. It was in this great hall that the Treaty of Versailles was signed in 1919 to signal the end of World War I .

The palace's private and public residences are now open to the public, including the Grand Apartment designed to honor Louis XIV as the Sun King—seven planets are the topic of paintings placed in the apartment's seven salons. The Grand Apartment also housed Venice's gift of *Christ at Supper with Simon* by Veronese.

Rich marble and bronze decor is a feature throughout the palace, and it comes as no surprise to learn that Louis XIV spent half of France's yearly income on making Versailles one of the most opulent and luxurious palaces in the world.

Eiffel Tower, FRANCE

Synonymous with the French capital and the world's biggest tourist attraction, the Eiffel Tower was conceived of as the entrance arch to the Exposition Universelle (World Fair) of 1889. The fair, host to 28 million visitors, aimed to show arts and crafts from around the globe as well as bringing scientific discoveries and agricultural and industrial innovations to the fore.

At the time of the tower's conception, architecture featuring the strength and beauty of iron was coming into its own (the huge Firth of Forth Bridge in Scotland was nearing completion, for example). This was the climate in which engineer and bridge builder Gustave Eiffel devised the tower in 1885. He brought in architect Stephen Sauvestre to make the design more acceptable to public opinion, and the result was one of the most memorable structures in world history.

At 986 ft (328 m) high the tower became the world's tallest structure when it was completed in 1889. It is still the tallest structure in Paris and a major landmark that dominates the skyline. Since its construction over 200 million people have visited the tower, and today it receives nearly 6.5 million visitors every year.

Gustave Eiffel designed the surface of the Tower to be exposed latticework supports made of iron, so that the wind had virtually nothing to grab onto.

Home to the world's most famous painting—Leonardo da Vinci's *Mona Lisa*—the Louvre in Paris ranks as one of the top repositories of art in existence. The building was originally conceived as a fortress in the 12th century, and was turned into a royal palace in the 16th century. However, today, with over eight million visitors annually, it is the most visited art gallery and museum in the world.

A castle was built on the site of the Louvre for the first time in 1190, but the basis of the current building was not constructed there until Renaissance architect Pierre Lescot designed the Château du Louvre in 1535.

Subsequent rulers, among them Louis XIII and Napoleon I, enhanced and updated the buildings right up to 1876. More recent additions include the Louvre Pyramid, designed by I. M. Pei, an elaborate glass structure over the entrance, commissioned by former president François Mitterrand in 1989 and the Inverted Pyramid, a breathtaking glass skylight designed to bring light down into the Louvre's underground complex. After dark, the pyramid is picked out by a frieze of lights and mirrors which also acts as an enormous chandelier.

Within its 6 miles (10 km) of galleries, the Louvre holds tens of thousands of works of art from around the world, the most celebrated of which include the iconic *Venus de Milo*, the ancient Greek statue dedicated to the goddess of love and beauty, attributed to Alexandros of Antioch. The museum also houses collections by well-known artists such as Rembrandt and Rubens, and—apart from the enigmatic *Mona Lisa*—other world-renowned paintings, such as *Saint Francis of Assisi Receives the Stigmata* by the Florentine painter Giotto (c. 1300), the *Ship of Fools* by Hieronymous Bosch (1490–1500), and *Liberty Leading the People* by Eugène Delacroix (1830), which famously shows the bold figure of a woman carrying the tricolor flag during the July Revolution of 1830.

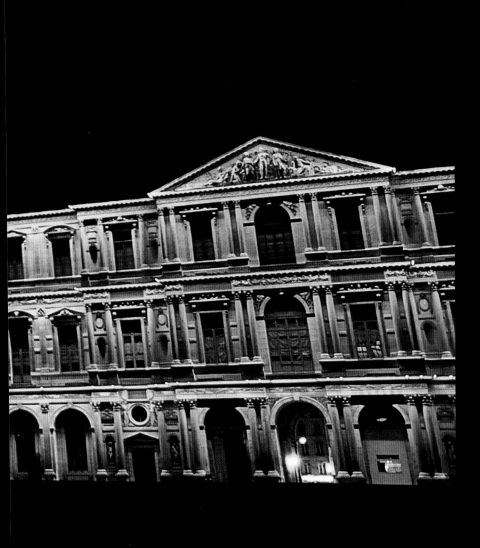

Millau Viaduct, FRANCE

About 45 ft (15 m) higher than the Eiffel Tower, the engineering wonder that is Millau Viaduct in southern France soars to 1,029 ft (343 m), enabling it in 2004 to snatch the title of the world's highest vehicular bridge from the Europabrücke in Austria, which had held the title since 1963.

Inspired by the Eiffel Tower, the Millau Viaduct comprises seven soaring concrete pillars, the highest of which is 1,029 ft (343 m) above the River Tarn.

Jointly created by British architect Norman Foster and French bridge engineer Michel Virlogeux, Millau was designed as a toll bridge to cut congestion in the River Tarn valley and ease traffic on the route from Paris to Spain via the Languedoc region.

The bridge measures an immense 7,380 ft (2,460 m) in length and took three years to construct. It comprises an eight-section bridge supported by colossal piers: the effect of the bridge against its beautiful backdrop is awe-inspiring and many people pull over to the viewing spot to appreciate the panorama and to take photographs.

Costing 394 million euros to construct, the bridge also necessitated the building of a toll plaza, pushing up the cost by an additional 20 million euros. The toll money is currently collected by the private building company responsible for the bridge, but the intention is for the French government eventually to assume control of it.

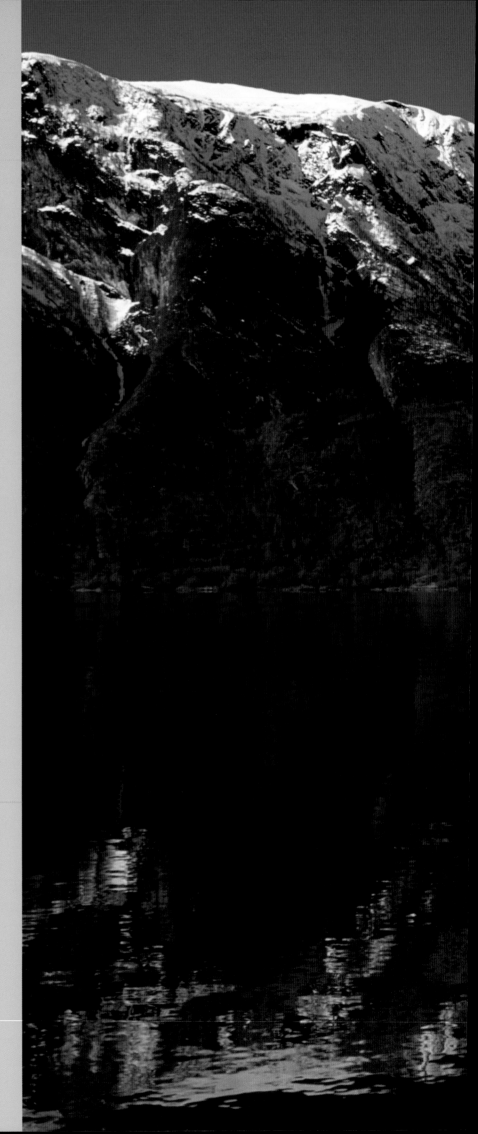

Fjords of Norway,
EUROPE

Carved gradually by glaciers over a period of three million years, Norway's fjords (sea inlets) are some of the longest, deepest, and narrowest in existence, and also offer some of the most spectacular natural scenery on earth. Although Norway boasts thousands of fjords, the three most well-known are Sognefjord, Hardangerfjord, and Storfjord.

Norway's fjords were formed during various ice ages by glaciers retreating from the land to the sea. They left behind steep-sided, U-shaped valleys whose floors extended well below sea level and were consequently filled by seawater.

At over 125 miles (200 km) in length, Sognefjord is the world's longest fjord; it also reaches depths of more than 3,900 ft (1,300 m), and the surrounding mountains (the

tallest in Norway) extend up to 5,100 ft (1,700 m). Just 40 miles (65 km) north of Bergen, Sognefjord's scenery embraces huge snow-capped mountain ranges and blue glaciers, as well as lush green hillsides and spectacular waterfalls (including some of Norway's highest) resulting from the thawing snow in May. The highest waterfall at 825 ft (275 m) is Vettisfossen, accessible to walkers up the scenic Utladalen in Ovre Ardal.

Some of the longest, deepest, narrowest, and most beautiful fjords in the world can be found along the entire length of the west coast of Norway.

Matterhorn, EUROPE

Famed for the shape of its peak rather than its size, the Matterhorn is nonetheless the seventh highest mountain in the Alps, rising up to 13,434 ft (4,478 m) on the Italian–Swiss border near the village of Zermatt.

The distinctive peak of the Matterhorn, which today is one of the most popular destinations in Europe for mountaineers.

For centuries the mountain was deemed impossible to climb. However, a party of seven mountaineers headed by Briton Edward Whymper finally reached the summit in 1865. Unfortunately, four members of the group perished in an accident during their descent.

Today it is one of the most popular mountains in Europe's ranges, with 3,000 climbers attempting to scale its heights every year.

The Matterhorn's pyramidal peak presents a face to each of the four compass directions and thus constitutes a distinctive mountain summit that is recognizable worldwide. It was created about 90 million years ago by the movement of the African tectonic plate over the European one.

Known as Mont Cervin in French and as Monte Cervino in Italian, the Matterhorn is thought to derive from the German words for "meadow" and "peak". By any name, the Matterhorn is one of the world's most beautiful mountains.

Marrakesh,
MOROCCO

Famed for Djamaa el Fna, its vibrant main square dubbed the most exhilarating meeting place in the world, Marrakesh in southwest Morocco also features a landmark symbol in its walled old city (*medina*): the 800-year-old minaret of the Koutoubia Mosque.

Snake charmers and Gnaouan drums pulse constantly from Djamaa el Fna Square, the most exuberant marketplace in the world.

The minaret, capped with three golden orbs, not only dominates the Marrakesh skyline but also enhances the mosque's reputation as a masterpiece of Islamic architecture. It was completed during the rule of Almohad Caliph Yacoub el-Mansour (1184–199) and stands nearly 230 ft (77 m) high and almost 40 ft (13 m) wide.

The city's character is, however, defined by Djamaa el Fna in the city's *medina* quarter. By day it is the scene of locals and tourists haggling for bargains with market traders and watching snake charmers. The *souk* (or marketplace) bordering the square is the largest in North Africa; its alleyways are crammed with stalls selling carpets and other Morrocan craft items.

By night the main square is transformed into a mesmerizing scene of street entertainment of every kind: fire-eating, juggling, singing, acrobatics, story-telling, dancing, magic, and stalls selling traditional medicines or spicy Moroccan dishes.

Leaning Tower of Pisa, ITALY

The celebrated precarious Italian structure is in fact Pisa Cathedral's separate bell tower. A Romanesque marvel that seems to present an optical illusion, it is located in the city's Campo dei Mirocoli (meaning "Field of Miracles"), an area of Pisa renowned for medieval art and the site of three other magnificent religious buildings: the Duomo (cathedral), the Baptistery, and the Camposanto (walled cemetery).

The tower was constructed in three phases that together span a total of 200 years. Although it is known that work started on the first floor in 1173, the identity of the building's architect remains a mystery. The tower began to lean five years later when the third floor was finished. Subsequently, no work was done for another hundred years.

Giovanni di Simone, the architect of the Camposanto, oversaw the second phase of the tower's construction with the addition of four further floors in 1272, which were built at an angle to try to rectify the tilt. The tower was not finally completed until 1372 when Tommaso di Andrea Pisano constructed a belfry on the seventh floor.

The belfry contains seven bells; the latest addition was the San Ranieri, cast in 1719–21 by Giovanni Andrea Moreni.

Over the centuries several remedies have been tried to rectify the tower's tilt, but none has been wholly successful. Indeed, the attempt by the Italian dictator Benito Mussolini in 1934, which involved pouring concrete into the foundations, actually made the tower subside further. However, the latest rescue plan, carried out at the end of last century, at a cost of US$ 30 million, has made the tower more stable, even though it continues to lean in the familiar way that makes it seem as though it will topple at any moment.

Over the centuries several remedies have been tried to rectify the tower's tilt.

Neuschwanstein Castle, GERMANY

A fairytale castle set against an idyllic backdrop of the Alps, Neuschwanstein is the breathtaking result of the whimsy of "Mad" King Ludwig II of Bavaria, Germany, and possibly the most famous castle in the world. The castle represents a romanticized version of a medieval fortress that has subsequently provided the inspiration for many film and cartoon versions of the dream castle, as well as for the Sleeping Beauty Castle at Disneyland.

Conceived of as a fanciful retreat from public life, Schloss Neuschwanstein (which translates literally as "New Swan Stone Castle") was commissioned by the reclusive king, Ludwig II (1845–1886). Ludwig had ascended the throne of Bavaria in 1864 at the age of 18 and, already considered eccentric, increasingly lived in a fantasy world. This culminated in his work with the set designer at the Court Theater in Munich, Christian Jank; together they started to build fairytale castles in the Alps from about 1880.

Work on Neuschwanstein started in 1869 and its completion took 23 years. On the outside it was a medieval fortress in the Germanic late Romanesque style of the 13th century; its interior was a mix of Gothic and Byzantine styles with modern comforts such as air central heating. It was not completed before Ludwig's death, although the king spent 11 nights in the unfinished castle in late spring 1884.

Of the castle's 360 rooms, only 14 have ever been decorated. Nonetheless, the castle is home to many wall paintings which recall scenes from the operas of Richard Wagner based on medieval legends, including the Grail King Parzival and Lohengrin (the Swan Knight for whom the castle is named). Ludwig idolized Wagner and had become his patron.

Ludwig was declared insane and deposed by his government in 1886. He drowned mysteriously in Lake Starnberg shortly afterward.

...the castle is home to many wall paintings which recall scenes from the operas of Richard Wagner...

Canals of Venice, ITALY

One of the most architecturally and culturally significant cities in the world—as well as one of the most romantic—Venice has been dubbed Italy's "City of Water" because instead of paved streets it has 150 canals as its main thoroughfares.

The city developed from the fifth century and is built on a collection of about 120 islands, joined by 400 bridges, including the famous Rialto Bridge. Venice's most famous crossing point, however, is the Ponte dei Sospiri (Bridge of Sighs), designed by Antonio Contino and constructed over the Rio di Palazzo in 1600 to link interrogation rooms in the Doge's palace with the prison. The "sighs" are said to be those of miscreants seeing the beautiful canals of Venice from the bridge before being condemned to imprisonment or death. Local lore has it that couples kissing in a gondola under the bridge at sunset will ensure the longevity of their love.

The city is mainly explored by foot and by water, either in the *vaporetti* (motorboat taxis) or the more celebrated *gondolas* (flat-bottomed boats powered by an oarsman that are generally left to romantic tourists).

Roads for land passenger vehicles are nonexistent in Venice so the 150 canals of the city function as its streets.

Most of Venice's significant architecture can be viewed from the water. Near the world-famous St. Mark's Square, for example, at the start of the Grand Canal (Venice's main thoroughfare) is the Santa Maria della Salute church, with its vast Baroque dome. The Grand Canal is bordered along its two-mile (3-km) length by elegant Renaissance buildings and *palazzi* (grand buildings) such as Ca' Rezzonico, Ca' d'Oro, and Palazzo Barbarigo.

Venice enjoys a fascinating mixture of architectural styles, including Byzantine, Neoclassical, Baroque, and Gothic, as evidenced in the façades of buildings on the canal sides or in the city's squares. The oldest building in Venice is believed to be the Basilica di Santa Maria dell'Assunta, constructed in 639 in the Byzantine style.

St. Mark's Basilica & Campanile, ITALY

Popularly known as the Church of Gold in reference to its lavish, highly gilded design, St. Mark's Basilica (Basilico di San Marco) in Venice is one of the world's finest examples of Byzantine architecture. The Campanile— the basilica's freestanding belltower—soars to an impressive 297 ft (99 m), ensuring its place as a major feature of the Venice skyline.

Famous for its elaborate mosaics and jewel-encrusted gilded altar screens, the current St. Mark's Basilica is the third version on this site. The first church dedicated to the saint and designed to accommodate his remains was built here in 832. The church was twice rebuilt before forming the basis of the current structure, which followed the Greek cross design of Justinian's Basilica of the Apostles in Constantinople. The church was consecrated in 1094, but its decoration has continued for centuries. Now Byzantine golden mosaics cover the interior walls and the building is rich with friezes and ornate carvings, often brought back from trips to the East, including the Fourth Crusade when Constantinople was conquered.

Watchtowers were built on the site of the belltower from the eighth century, and the first campanile was positioned there in 1514. The current campanile is the exact reconstruction, completed in 1912 of a tower that unexpectedly fell down in 1902. It features an observation level affording fine views over Venice's rooftops, and a section accommodating its famous five bells, including the *marangona*, which chimed in the morning and evening to indicate the start and finish of the working day. The tower is topped by a golden statue of the Archangel Gabriel, which rotates with the wind: when the statue faces the Basilica it is said that Venice will experience high water levels.

St. Peter's Basilica, ITALY

The Vatican City in Italy is home to the design and architectural masterpiece St. Peter's Basilica (Basilica di San Pietro). This 16th-century church, the largest in existence—it holds 60,000 people —is a focus for the world's estimated one billion Catholics, and its instantly recognizable dome makes it a major highlight of Rome's skyline.

St. Peter's Basilica was constructed on the site of an earlier church commissioned by Emperor Constantine in the fourth century. The location is deemed to be the burial place of chief apostle Saint Peter after his death in 64 CE. The first stone of the new basilica was laid by Pope Julius II in 1506 but the building was not completed until 1626—two years after the death of Michelangelo, its second chief architect.

Michelangelo designed the impressive ribbed dome— the world's largest—with a

From the top of the dome there is an unequalled view of Rome and the huge, elliptical St. Peter's square.

diameter of 126 ft (42 m) and a height of 414 ft (138 m). The opulent decoration of the basilica is the work of famous Renaissance and Baroque artists and architects, and includes Bernini's monumental Baroque Throne of St. Peter as well as Michelangelo's marble sculpture masterpiece of Pietà, which depicts Christ in his mother's arms after the crucifixion.

Michelangelo designed the impressive ribbed dome—the world's largest...

Sistine Chapel, ITALY

The Sistine Chapel not only contains Michelangelo's world-famous frescoed ceiling depicting God creating Adam, it also functions as the site at which a new Pope is selected, and is therefore both an artistic and a spiritual wonder.

The chapel was constructed between 1473 and 1484 at the behest of Pope Sixtus IV (after whom it was named). It forms part of the Papal Palace—the Pope's official residence in Vatican City—and was built to match the dimensions of the Temple of Solomon. It is most renowned for the Renaissance paintings created by Michelangelo on its 63-ft (21-m)-high ceiling between 1508 and 1512. The series of paintings depicts nine scenes from the Book of Genesis, including God creating Adam, which shows the hand of God giving life to Adam.

Michelangelo used the fresco method, which involves applying paint to damp plaster, and employed bright colors and broad outlines to ensure the images' visibility from the ground. The project took four years to complete. Nearly 20 years afterward he painted *The Last Judgment* behind the chapel altar, a six-year project. These paintings are among the most treasured frescoes in the world, and the chapel includes further works of great Renaissance painters, including Botticelli's *Temptation of Christ* and Perugino's *Christ Giving the Keys to St. Peter*.

Michelangelo used scaffolding, which was inserted into holes under the windows, to paint the ceiling.

These paintings are among the most treasured frescoes in the world...

The Colosseum, ITALY

The scene of Ancient Rome's most lavish and gory spectacles, the Colosseum is the world's best-known amphitheater. Audiences numbering up to 50,000 would be enthralled by gladiatorial contests, animal hunts, and other spectacles including games, dramas, battle reenactments, and executions.

Named for the nearby colossal statue of Nero which was believed to have magical powers, the Colosseum was designed as a massive entertainment center. It primarily hosted spectacles with gladiators—professional swordsmen who would do battle to the death with condemned prisoners and other gladiators for honor and possible freedom after three years (although average gladiatorial life expectancy was only one year).

Considered an architectural and engineering wonder, the Colosseum is proof of both the grandeur and the cruelty of the Roman world.

Wild animals were slaughtered in gladiatorial battles on a massive scale. Mostly imported from Africa, the animals included elephants, crocodiles, lions, and rhinoceros, and 11,000 of them were killed during the first 100 days celebrating the opening of the Colosseum.

The animals were hoisted into the arena by a system of ropes and pulleys from cages in the hypogeum (underground tunnels) below its 249 by 144ft (83 by 48 m) platform. The hypogeum was added to the original amphitheater, commissioned by Emperor Vespasian in 72 CE and completed during the reign of his son Titus in 80 CE. The building, which measured 144 ft (48 m) high, 468 ft (156 m) wide, and 567 ft (189 m) long, was the biggest in the Roman Empire.

Pompeii, ITALY

Hidden beneath a 30-ft (10-m) layer of volcanic debris for over 1,600 years, Pompeii in Italy was once a thriving city in Ancient Rome. When Mount Vesuvius erupted in 79 CE, lava rapidly covered the city` and effectively "froze" it in time. Today the excavated site offers an unprecedented vision of how everyday life must have been in Ancient Rome.

Pompeii boasted homes for about 20,000 people in addition to a food market, a mill, bars, and restaurants, an amphitheater, a *palaestra* (a sporting and educational establishment with a swimming pool), and a sophisticated aqueduct system that supplied water to the city's homes as well as public fountains and baths.

A highlight of Pompeii is the Villa of Mysteries, a remarkably well-preserved residence of a wealthy family with a wine press and fine rooms. It contains celebrated frescoes showing a woman being initiated in the cult of the god Dionysus.

Serious excavation of Pompeii began in 1860 under the guidance of Guiseppe Fiorelli, who surmised that gaps in the ash were spaces left by decomposed corpses. He flowed plaster into the spaces and the result is the familiar re-creations of the volcano's victims, some with visible expressions of horror frozen on their faces for all time.

A highlight of Pompeii is the Villa of Mysteries,
a remarkably well-preserved residence...

Delphi, GREECE

Located on the sacred mountain of Parnassus, Delphi was home to the most important oracle in the world and was considered by the Ancient Greeks to be the center of the universe. This archeological site ranks in world importance today because it is the site of the Temple of Apollo and the Tholos Temple, as well as of the treasuries of the Athenians and the Syphnians, and it was a stadium where the Pythian Games were held.

Legend has it that Apollo, god of music and prophecy, rid Delphi of its monstrous serpent (Python) and took charge of the prophetess it guarded, installing her in his temple. There she would inhale the fumes from a fissure in the earth to put her in a trance and, thus possessed by Apollo's spirit, she would make her prophecies. Subsequently the Temple of Apollo became the most important oracle center in Ancient Greece, with ordinary people consulting the prophetess on everyday matters, and rulers and military leaders consulting her on state affairs or wars.

As well as possessing votive statues brought by prophecy supplicants, Delphi boasts many treasuries (small shrines) donated in gratitude following military success predicted by the oracle.

The finest example is the Athenian treasury (490 BCE), created after success at the Battle of Marathon.

Delphi is also the site of the Tholos (a circular temple built in the Doric style), which was constructed to honor the goddess Athena in 380 BCE. Although only three of its original 20 columns remain, it is still a paragon of its type.

The Stadium hosted the Pythian Games in Apollo's honor every four years, beginning in the 6th century BCE. These games were a precursor of the Olympic Games, but also included music and poetry competitions.

...the Temple of Apollo became the most important oracle center in Ancient Greece...

The Parthenon & the Acropolis, GREECE

The Parthenon in Athens has served the Byzantines as a church, the Catholics as a cathedral, and the Turks as a mosque. However, the structure is the most important symbol of Ancient Greece. It was originally conceived as a temple dedicated to Athena (patron goddess of Athens, wisdom, war, the arts, industry, and justice) and is named for her (*Parthenon* means "dwelling of the maiden").

The temple was built at the height of the Greek Golden Age on the rocky outcrop of the Acropolis ("the high city"), which had been a site of temples and monuments in honor of gods for the previous 1,000 years. Perikles, a politician dubbed the founder of Athens and credited with ushering in the Golden Age, commissioned the sculptor Phidias to design the temple. Its purpose was to house a huge statue of Athena adorned with so much gold and ivory that today it would cost about US$ 12 million to produce.

Constructed between 447 and 438 BCE, the temple was made almost entirely of marble (previously temples were made of wood) and it measures nearly 90 by 210 ft (30 by 70 m). The result is one of the world's finest examples of the Doric style, the plainest of the classical Greek styles.

Still impressive, the Parthenon stood more or less intact as a place of worship until in 1687 an explosion tore through the building during a battle between the Turks and the Venetians.

Decorative sculptures completed in 432 BCE include scenes from Ancient Greek mythology, such as the battle of the Gigantes (Earth mother Gaia's giant children) with the Olympian gods; Athena's birth; and history, such as scenes from the Trojan War. A relief frieze on four sides of the building shows the Procession of Panathenea, a major religious festival in ancient Athens that ended with a procession to the temple and the sacrifice of one hundred oxen in honor of Athena, followed by a huge banquet.

Victoria Falls,
AFRICA

Famously brought to the West's attention by Scottish medical missionary and explorer Dr. David Livingstone, the thunderous Victoria Falls on Zimbabwe's border with Zambia present the largest individual cascade of water in the world.

One of the most visited spots in southern Africa, the falls are created where the Zambezi River arrives at a sheer gorge that is about 1 mile (1.6 km) wide and 324 ft (108 m) high—about twice the height of Niagara Falls on the US–Canada border.

The river continues for 50 miles (80 km) after Victoria Falls via a series of high gorges, the first of which includes a deep basin called the Boiling Pot, where the torrent rages at high water. Dr. Livingstone, the first westerner to report sighting the misty falls during his Zambezi expedition in 1855, named them for Queen Victoria. Tourism to the area subsequently became popular when a railway was built in 1905. Today the falls form part of both the Victoria National Park in Zimbabwe and the Mosi-oa-Tunya National Park in Zambia.

Nearly 19 million cubic feet (550 million cubic liters) of water cascade into the Fall's chasm every minute during the Zambezi River's peak flow.

...the falls are created where the Zambezi River arrives at a sheer gorge...

Hagia Sophia, TURKEY

Best known for its remarkable dome, the Hagia Sophia ("Church of Holy Wisdom") in Istanbul, Turkey, is a 6th-century Byzantine masterpiece. Originally commissioned as a Christian church by Emperor Justinian I, it was converted into a mosque in 1453 before finally becoming the Ayasofya Museum in 1935.

The emperor used four immense Corinthian columns plundered from Baalbek, Lebanon, in the church's construction. However, the major marvel of Hagia Sophia is its dome: nearly 168 ft (56 m) high and 93 ft (31 m) in diameter, its erection was an astonishing architectural feat for its time. The combination of a series of 40 arched windows below it and four pendentives to support it gives the impression that the dome is floating. The dome adds to the building's mysticism and the church's importance as the center of Eastern Christianity in the Byzantine period up to the Ottoman conversion.

When the Ottomans conquered Istanbul (then named Constantinople) in 1453, ruler Mehmed II reconsecrated Hagia Sophia as the Ayasofya Mosque. Over the next hundred years the Christian mosaics of angels, saints, and seraphims were covered with plaster or paint, and four towering minarets were added to the building.

In contrast to the simple exterior, the interior walls of Hagia Sophia are covered in colorful marble plaques blended with mosaics.

...the major marvel of Hagia Sophia is its dome: nearly 168 ft (56 m) high...

Abu Simbel, EGYPT

Hewn from a sandstone cliff in southern Egypt, Abu Simbel comprises two outstanding temples commissioned by Pharaoh Ramses II to honor himself and his wife, Queen Nefertari, in the 13th century BCE. The Great Temple is famous for the four colossal 60-ft (20-m) high statues of Ramses guarding its entrance.

Constructed between 1284 and 1264 BCE, these masterpieces of Egyptian architecture were designed to emphasize Egypt's religious and political power in the region. The Great Temple, dedicated to Ramses II and the three gods Amun, Ra, and Ptah, includes a grand hall, several chapels, and a façade that features 22 sun-worshiping baboons. (Baboons were believed to help the sun god Ra conquer night's darkness and so were regarded as sacred.)

The Great Temple's magnificent façade is dominated by four enormous seated statues of the Pharaoh, each over 60 ft (20 m) high.

Over time the temples were forgotten because of their remote location and eventually they were largely buried in sand. However, in 1813 they were rediscovered by Italian explorer Giovanni Battista Belzoni, who cleared the sand from the temples, and brought them to the attention of the West.

In the 1960s the reservoir created by the construction of the Aswan High Dam threatened to flood the site. An international team of engineers and archeologists joined forces to relocate the temples nearly 200 ft (65 m) above the water level, thereby saving them from destruction.

Pyramids of Giza, EGYPT

Ranking as the tallest structure on earth for over 4,000 years, the Great Pyramid of Giza near Cairo is a potent symbol of Ancient Egypt that still has the power to amaze and fascinate visitors in the modern world.

The ancient remains of the Giza necropolis have attracted visitors and tourists since classical antiquity, when these Old Kingdom monuments were already over 2,000 years old.

The pyramid is an astonishing and enigmatic feat of construction. Soaring to over 400 ft (135 m) high, it contains more than two million stone blocks that, laid end to end, would create a wall 9 ft (3 m) high around the perimeter of France. The base of the pyramid is about 690 ft^2 (230 m^2)—that's about the area of twelve soccer fields. Not surprisingly, this colossal building has provoked much debate about its method of construction and its purpose.

Completed in 2560 BCE, the Great Pyramid is the oldest and largest of three on the Giza Plateau, and it is believed to have taken between 20,000 and 100,000 workers at least 20 years to complete. Its function has been variously thought to be an astronomical observatory and a cult temple, but its most convincing purpose is as the tomb of Pharaoh Khufu, who ruled Ancient Egypt between 2589 and 2566 BCE. Incorporating corridors, galleries, and escape shafts, the immense structure's centerpiece is the king's burial chamber, which houses Khufu's red granite sarcophagus.

Karnak Temple,
EGYPT

Famed for its immense statues, avenues of ram-headed sphinxes, and towering structures, the Temple of Karnak in Luxor, Egypt, was the religious headquarters of the Ancient Egyptians and the largest ancient religious complex on the planet. It includes the spectacular Great Hypostyle Hall in the Temple of Amon-Ra.

Construction took place during the reigns of 30 pharaohs but most of the work was carried out during the New Kingdom period (1570–1100 BCE). At this time the site was combined with Luxor to form Egypt's capital, Waset (later named Thebes by the Ancient Greeks).

Beautifully carved hieroglyphics and designs cover the Hall's columns.

The Temple of Amon-Ra is the most significant building of the complex, sufficiently vast to contain London's Westminster Abbey twice. Amon-Ra came to be worshiped over time as the father of the gods and a sun god. Together with his consort Mut and their son Khonsu (replacing a previous son Menthu), they formed the main triad of gods who were worshiped at Karnak.

A major highlight of the site is the Great Hypostyle Hall. Commissioned under Pharaoh Seti I (1294–1279 BCE) and completed under the rule of Ramses II (1279–1213 BCE), it contained 134 colossal columns soaring to almost 100 ft (33 m) and decorated with fine carvings and paintings. The hall acted as a vestibule between the courtyard and smaller inner sacred rooms of the temple.

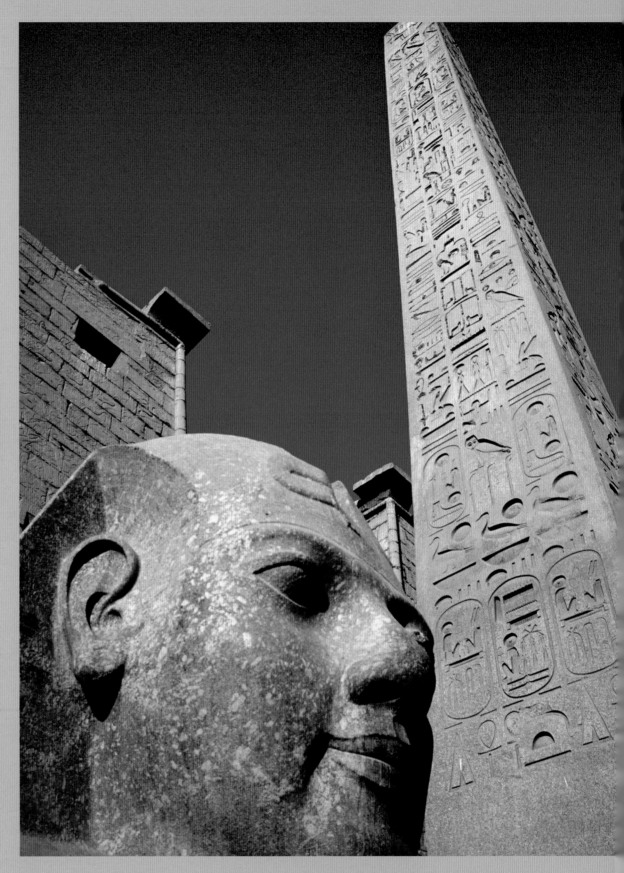

Construction took place during the reigns of 30 pharaohs...

Valley of the Kings, EGYPT

Internationally renowned as the location of the remarkably well-preserved tomb of Pharaoh Tutankhamun, the Valley of the Kings near Luxor in Egypt was the graveyard for the country's great and good between the 16th and 11th centuries BCE. Today it is one of the most popular sites on the planet for the living, attracting over 9,000 visitors every day.

The valley contains at least 63 tombs, carved up to 360 ft (120 m) into the rock and then sealed. Some tombs—particularly that of Seti I (1278 BCE)—are highly decorated with fine bas-reliefs and colorful paintings, including images of the falcon-headed sun god Ra.

The first tombs belonged to Amenhotep I (1506 BCE) and Thutmose I (1493 BCE), and the last known one belonged to Ramses X (1102 BCE)—although it is disputed whether he was ever actually entombed there.

The most famous of the burial sites in the valley was discovered by British archeologist Howard Carter in 1922: the tomb of Tutankhamun. It was so crammed with artefacts that it took ten years to catalog and move them to Cairo's Egyptian Museum.

Items such as Tutankhamun's solid gold funerary mask have achieved worldwide recognition as icons of Ancient Egypt and indeed have been displayed all around the globe. An exhibition in 1972 at the British Museum in London was the most popular ever mounted at the museum, attracting 1.6 million visitors.

It is ironic that in life Tutankhamun was one of Egypt's least important Pharaohs and yet in death has become one of the most significant. He was a boy king: he came to power in 1333 BCE at the age of nine and ruled only until 1324 BCE. It is more than likely that important acts carried out during his reign, such as the reinstatement of the traditional pantheon of Egyptian gods and the erection of many temples, were instigated by his advisors rather than by the king himself.

...the tomb of Tutankhamun ...was so crammed with artefacts that it took ten years to catalog...

The Aswan High Dam, EGYPT

The biggest dam on the globe, the Aswan High Dam redirects the water of the Nile River in Egypt to create Lake Nasser, the largest artificial lake in the world. The purpose of the dam is to provide hydroelectric power for the whole country, control flooding of the Nile, and supply water for agriculture.

The dam supports the work of Aswan Low Dam, which was initially constructed in 1902 and subsequently increased in height twice. Construction on the Aswan High Dam started in 1960 under the government of President Gamal Abdel Nasser (1918–1970) and was completed ten years later at a cost of US$ 1 billion.

Named for the president, the vast Lake Nasser is nearly 310 miles (500 km) long, over 12 miles (20 km wide), and nearly 300 ft (100 m) deep. It began to take water from the redirected river in 1964, requiring the relocation of up to 120,000 people and the moving of many monuments (including the colossal rock temples at Abu Simbel).

The dam itself is 364 ft (121 m) tall and almost 2.4 miles (3.8 km) long (that's about 12 Eiffel Towers laid end-to-end). Over 14,000 cubic yards (11,000 cubic meters) of water can pass through its generators every second. Six 45-ft (15-m) wide tunnels direct water to the front of the dam, and 180 water gates and 12 generators can produce more than 2.1 million kW of electric power.

...180 water gates and 12 generators can produce
more than 2.1 million kW of electric power.

St. Basil's Cathedral, RUSSIA

Designed to celebrate Ivan the Terrible's defeat of the Tartar Mongols in 1552, St. Basil's Cathedral is an extravagant and arresting feature located near the Kremlin in Red Square, Moscow, Russia, and its onion-style domes make it one of the world's most instantly recognizable buildings.

The architect Postnik Yakovlev incorporated nine chapels in the cathedral's design, each capped with an unusual brightly colored onion-style dome that gives the building its distinctive appearance. The domes form a symbolic eight-pointed star around a central spire, considered to represent the Christian Church as the guiding light of humankind.

Ivan the Terrible originally named the building the Cathedral of Intercession of the Virgin on the Moat.

However, it acquired its present name from Basil the Blessed when Tsar Fedor Ivanovich added a chapel to the building in his honor in 1588. From a humble birth in Yelokhov near Moscow in 1468, Vasily Blazhenny grew up to be canonized as Basil the Blessed (or Basil Fool for Christ) in about 1580 following his death in 1552. Much loved by Muscovites, Basil was thought to be a "holy fool," an eccentric who stole from shops to give to the poor.

Each of the cathedral's nine domes has a distinctive patterning and color scheme, creating a stunning effect. The extravagant exterior masks a much more modestly decorated interior.

The domes form a symbolic eight-pointed star around a central spire...

Kremlin, RUSSIA

Commanding views of Red Square and the Moskva River, the Kremlin is Russia's premier citadel, a wondrous walled fortress complex containing palaces, armories, and cathedrals in the heart of Moscow.

Moscow became the seat of the Russian Orthodox Church under Saint Peter, Metropolitan of Moscow and all Russia, in 1320 when he transferred power from Kiev. Subsequently Ivan the Great (1462–1505) led the expansion of Muscovite rule over the whole of Russia and the establishment of the Kremlin as the seat of power under the Tsars until Peter the Great selected St. Petersburg (now Leningrad) as the capital in 1703. Power shifted back to Moscow in 1918 after the Bolshevik Revolution of 1917.

The Kremlin today is home to an extraordinary array of medieval and modern buildings. The Arsenal was originally commissioned by Peter the Great to house weapons and currently the Kremlin Guard is stationed here.

The State Kremlin Palace was constructed in 1961 under President Khruschev as an imposing auditorium for party conferences, but it now stages performances of the Kremlin Ballet Company.

The neoclassical Senate building, commissioned from architect Matvey Kazakov by Catherine the Great in 1776, now functions as the Russian President's residence. Considered an architectural masterpiece, the structure's Round Hall was known as "the Russian Pantheon." Nearly 100 ft (33 m) high and 82 ft (27m) in diameter, the hall features a Corinthian colonnade, bas-reliefs, and a vault containing 24 windows.

Other highlights of the Kremlin include the Tsar Cannon and Bell (both the world's largest, but strangely never used); Cathedral Square (location of the splendid Cathedral of the Assumption, 1470, and other cathedrals, towers, and palaces representing Tsarist Russia at its architectural finest); and the Ivan the Great Belltower, a sparkling golden dome that dominates the Kremlin and that was Russia's tallest structure for years.

The Kremlin today is home to an extraordinary array of medieval and modern buildings.

Aurora Borealis

The Aurora Borealis is nature's answer to the most spectacular firework display you have ever witnessed. An atmospheric phenomenon seen around the North Pole, it comprises rays of green, red, blue, and violet light that form vast phosphorescent curtains, which disappear and reform as they twirl across the night sky.

Also known as the Northern Lights because it occurs in the Northern Hemisphere, Aurora Borealis means "red dawn of the north." (Aurora is the Roman Goddess of the dawn, and Boreas is Greek for north wind.) The lights would primarily have appeared as a red horizon (like a sunrise in the wrong direction) to Italian scientist Galileo Galilei (1564–1642), who named the lights Aurora Borealis.

Aurora Borealis is most frequently seen around the spring and fall equinoxes, but in the auroral zone near the North Pole a version of the lights can be observed on most clear winter nights. At their most intense, the lights can produce the same kind of light as a full moon, allowing the spectator a view of the landscape or sufficient light to read by.

The phenomenon is caused by particles from the sun colliding with gases in the earth's atmosphere to produce photons (light particles). It occurs near the North Pole because the sun's particles are attracted and guided to this point by the earth's magnetic field. The lights can be viewed from northern parts of Norway, Sweden, Denmark, Finland, Iceland, and Greenland, as well as north of Alaska, USA, and northern parts of Canada and Russia.

Appearing as a diffuse glow or as flickering curtains of dancing light, which can evolve and change, the Aurora Borealis is one of the most spectacular of nature's phenomena.

At their most intense, the lights can produce the same kind of light as a full moon...

The Northern Red Sea, EGYPT

Often referred to as an "Underwater Garden of Eden," the northern Red Sea area of Ras Muhammad near Sharm el-Sheikh in Egypt is a marine-based National Park that is home to some of the most beautiful coral beds and colorful sealife anywhere on earth.

One reason for the rich diversity of marine life in the Red Sea's northern reaches is the region's exceptionally clear sky; intense sunlight provides abundant solar energy for the corals, and the fish who rely on them.

The reef teems with aquatic flora and fauna: it contains over 200 types of coral as well as many hundreds of species of tropical fish, sea urchins, molluscs, crustaceans, and starfish. Sealife in these waters originates from both the Atlantic and Pacific Oceans because of shifts in the earth's tectonic plates opening and closing the Red Sea to outside influence over millions of years.

The reef's soft corals appear to glow in the sunlight—from green to red to yellow—and some species of sea anemone are also illuminated a striking orange color, owing to the presence of algae. Many divers explore the so-called "Anemone City," a reef containing a myriad white and green tentacled anemones, as well as gaudy Clown Fish and spotty Domino Fish.

Fishermen's Bank is another popular dive site, because its caves and caverns are home to many colorful reef fish, such as the Bluecheek Butterflyfish, the bright-red Lionfish with its poisonous spines, stingrays, and varieties of Angelfish.

Jerusalem Old City,
ISRAEL

The Old City of Jerusalem has come to be held as sacred by Christians, Jews, and Muslims during its 3,000-year history. Within this walled labyrinthine plot of land are some of the holiest, most architecturally esthetic sites in the world, including the Via Dolorosa, the Wailing Wall, and the Dome of the Rock.

Divided into four unequally sized districts, the Old City comprises the Armenian, Christian, Jewish, and Muslim quarters, but there are sites significant to the main religions located throughout the city.

For Christians, Old Jerusalem is the site of the Via Dolorosa (the "Way of Sorrows"), purported to be the road on which Jesus carried his cross to Calvary. The Church of the Holy Sepulcher, which commemorates the death, burial, and resurrection of Jesus Christ, and which is said to be on the site of his crucifixion, is also here.

For Jews, the holiest feature of the city is the Western Wall, or Kotel—more commonly known as the "Wailing Wall." It is the remnant of an outer wall surrounding the Temple Mount, the site of the first two (now destroyed) Jewish temples in Jerusalem.

According to Jewish tradition, the coming of the Messiah will see the building of the third and final temple on this site. The prayers of Jews visiting the wall to lament the destruction of the temples were so passionate that onlookers devised the term "Wailing Wall." As well as praying, people offer messages and prayers (*kvitlach*) in paper form and insert them into holes in the wall.

To Muslims, the Temple Mount area is known as Haram es-Sharif (the "Noble Enclosure"). It contains two 7th-century shrines: the Dome of the Rock, an Islamic sanctuary and Byzantine architectural masterpiece, and the al-Aksa mosque. After Mecca and Medina, Muslims consider the site to be their third holiest in the world, primarily because the *Koran* says that it is from here that Muhammed ascended to heaven.

Petra, JORDAN

The ancient city of Petra in Jordan—renowned for its magnificent temples and tombs—was hewn from sandstone rock by nomadic Nabataean Arabs in the 6th century BCE. The city was abandoned after an earthquake in 363 CE, and its rediscovery is credited to Swiss explorer Johann Ludwig Burckhardt, who brought its splendid ruins to the West's attention in 1812.

Although remote, Petra originally developed because of its position on ancient trade routes. The city was easily defended—it is surrounded by mountains and its main entrance is via the Siq, a narrow gorge that in places shrinks to little over 6 ft (2 m) wide. In addition, the Nabataeans devised a sophisticated water supply system that included conduits along the Siq.

The most impressive ruin at Petra is Al Khazneh ("the Treasury"), so-called because local Bedouins believed the urn at the summit of the edifice (140 ft/47 m high) contained treasure. However, like the rest of the building, the urn is carved from solid sandstone and Al Khazneh was more probably used as a temple and/or tomb.

The city also boasts an amphitheater (designed to seat 8,000 people for speeches by city leaders or performances of plays); tombs carved out of the rock; and freestanding structures including a restored temple known as "The Castle of Pharaoh's Daughter," and a priest building close to a high plateau where animal sacrifices took place.

The city also boasts an amphitheater (designed to seat 8,000 people)...

Baalbek, LEBANON

Home to some of the most ornate and imposing Ancient Roman ruins in the world, Baalbek presents itself and its rich and enigmatic history as a sacred site in the Bekaa Valley, about 50 miles (80 kilometers) from Lebanon's capital city, Beirut.

Primarily known for its time as Heliopolis ("City of the Sun") under the Ancient Romans, Baalbek prides itself on a temple complex commissioned by Emperor Augustus in 27 CE. The site includes three of the finest examples of Roman religious structures known to exist, namely, the temples of Jupiter (the Great Temple), Bacchus (the Little Temple), and Venus (the Round Temple).

The Temple of Jupiter is thought to be the biggest sacred structure of the Roman Empire. Six of its 54 original colossal Corinthian columns remain to provide the site's trademark feature. At 72 ft (24 m) high the columns dominate the Baalbek skyline and, coupled with the dimensions of the temple's enormous base—288 by 156 ft (96 by 52 m)—suggest the immense size of the building that once was.

The temple stands on a podium built with some of the most massive carved blocks ever

used—most weighing 300 tons each. Three of the stones —known as the Trilothon— weigh about 800 tons apiece.

The origin of these stones is controversial: some experts believe they were carved and positioned in megalithic times. Even by Roman times there were no known means of moving gigantic blocks that measure 65 by about 15 ft (22 by 5 m), and some have suggested their presence indicates a lost civilization more highly advanced than currently believed possible.

Baalbek's temples were all abandoned under the rule of Byzantine Emperor Constantine when Christianity became the official Roman religion in 313 CE. Emperor Theodosius had a basilica built in the Great Court of the Jupiter Temple at the end of the fourth century CE to consolidate the importance of the new religion, and the ruins of this building are still evident to this day.

The temple stands on a podium built with some of the most massive carved blocks ever used...

Serengeti Migration,
AFRICA

The world's most spellbinding wildlife event takes place every year on the vast plains and grasslands of East Africa. The Serengeti migration sees about 1.5 million wildebeest, zebras, and gazelles on a clockwise, circular journey that takes them over 1,860 miles (3,000 km) across the far-reaching Serengeti plains of Tanzania to the gentle rolling hills and woodland of the Masai Mara in Kenya and back again.

The migrating herbivores (1.4 million wildebeest and 200,000 zebras and gazelles) are seeking water and grass that appear in different areas of the region according to the season. They encounter many hazards en route, including predatory animals and geographical obstacles, such as the Mara River.

In addition, about 400,000 wildebeest calves are born between January and March, at the onset of this great journey when the herds are generally gathering in the southern Serengeti. Lions, hyenas, and cheetahs are a constant threat at this point.

In April and May the herds abandon the now sparse plains and head for the woodland and long-grass plains of Serengeti's Western Corridor near Lake Victoria. In June the animals seek fresh pastures in the north towards the Lamai Wedge and the Mara Triangle. In July the herds gather by the Mara River. If they are lucky the river is low and they cross easily, but often animals drown in the current or fall prey to crocodiles. The successful ones reside in the Masai Mara, grazing on its short grasses until the end of October, when they return to the southern Serengeti.

Ngorongoro Crater, TANZANIA

The largest intact volcanic crater in the world, the Ngorongoro Crater in northern Tanzania is set in scenic grandeur and is home to over 25,000 animals, including zebras, wildebeest, black rhino, lions, and elephants, making it a peerless destination for safaris.

The crater is ringed with steep walls, and shelters forests, grasslands, fresh springs, and a large soda lake. Since most of the crater floor is grassland, grazing animals such as zebra, gnu, gazelles, buffalo, eland, and warthogs predominate.

The crater, which is almost 1,970 ft (700 m) deep and 100 square miles (260 km²) in surface area, was created over two million years ago. Formerly a volcano the size of Mount Kilimanjaro, it collapsed in on itself after an eruption and the crater was formed.

Today Ngorongoro provides year-round pasture and water in the form of forest areas, grassland, swamps, and Lake Magadi, a soda lake in the center of the crater floor, which teems with flamingos and other waterbirds.

The crater's steep walls tend to ensure animals do not migrate (as they do on the nearby Serengeti plains), and in fact the constant pasture and water means that migration is unnecessary.

Given that it provides a natural enclosure for one of the densest concentrations of wildlife in East Africa, including the endangered black rhino and herds of buffalo, it is not surprising that increasing numbers of people—all hoping to see a rhinoceros, lion, or leopard—are visiting the crater on safari.

Mount Kilimanjaro,
TANZANIA

To climb Mount Kilimanjaro in Tanzania, East Africa, is to pass through steamy equatorial rainforest, moorland, and alpine desert to arrive at a snowy summit with breathtaking views of the Great Rift Valley. According to legend, it is the birthplace of humankind; at the very least it is the highest point in the whole of Africa and the tallest freestanding mountain in the world.

Kilimanjaro (Swahili for "shining mountain") is a dormant volcano that soars to 19,340 ft (6,447 m). The volcano comprises three cones: Shira, Mawenzi, and Kibo. Kibo, which includes the highest point (Uhuru Peak), produces sulfur and steam, and boasts a crater that has a diameter of almost 1.3 miles (2 km).

Historically, few attempts would have been made to ascend the mountain. It first came to European attention in 1848 when German missionary Johann Rebmann sighted it while traversing the Tsavo plains. Johannes Kinyala Lauwo, a local Marangu army scout, ascended the mountain several times before acting as guide to a German expedition led by Dr. Hans Meyer. Meyer's expedition took six weeks to become the first nonindigenous climbing group to reach the summit in October 1889.

The mountain has become a popular destination for climbers—over 1,000 people made the ascent to watch the millennium sunrise in 2000—but these days the average climber takes only one week to reach its lofty summit.

Mecca, SAUDI ARABIA

The birthplace of Muhammed and the most sacred city in Islam, Mecca is situated near Jeddah, some 50 miles (80 km) from Saudi Arabia's Red Sea coast. It is home to the largest Islamic structure in the world, the Sacred Mosque (Al-Masjid al-Haram), which is built around the shrine of Kaaba, the centerpiece of Mecca.

The Sacred Mosque is crowned with seven soaring minarets, has 64 gates, and covers an area of nearly 4 million ft^2 (370,000 m^2). It is able to accommodate 820,000 worshipers at a time, which is vital given that the month of pilgrimage (*Hajj*) sees about four million of the world's 1.3 billion Muslims visiting Mecca every year. (All Muslims whose finances and health allow them are expected to make the *Hajj* to Mecca at least once during their lives.)

Mecca developed as a pilgrimage site for Muslims when Muhammed (570–632 CE) and his followers took posession of the city in 630 and in so doing assumed control of the Kaaba, a shrine said to have been built by Abraham and his son Ishmael at God's instruction.

Today the Kaaba is the holiest Islamic shrine in the world. Muslims pray five times a day and wherever they are in the world they turn to face the direction of the Kaaba. The Kaaba (meaning "cube" in Arabic) is a square granite building on a marble base: its sides measure 34 by 40 ft (11 by 13 m). It is shrouded in the *kiswah*, a black curtain with golden sacred text from the *Koran*, and one of its cornerstones is the revered Black Stone. Some pilgrims try to kiss this stone when performing the ritual circumambulations (*tawaf*) of the Kaaba during their *Hajj* or *Umrah* (lesser pilgrimage) visit; others use it as a marker to help them keep track of the number of times they have walked around the Kaaba.

Today the Kaaba is the holiest Islamic shrine in the world.

Throne Hall of Persepolis, IRAN

A former capital of the Persian Empire (now known as Iran), Persepolis was the cultural, political, and military hub of an ancient superpower—with architecture to match. Today the ruins of this palace complex are some of the most awe-inspiring on the globe.

The immense Throne Hall, also known as the Palace of One Hundred Columns, includes a 230-ft^2 (77-m^2) throne room, dates from the 5th century BCE and is one of the highlights of the site. Its 100 columns were made of wood and have disintegrated, but their stone bases are intact. Fine reliefs of throne scenes and images of Xerxes I (ruler of Persia between 485 and 465 BCE) doing battle with mythical beasts adorn its stone entrances. Two immense carved bulls guard the portico.

The Throne Hall functioned as a state reception room, and was a particularly important showpiece in a complex designed not just as a residence but also as a spectacular venue for the royal festivities. The new year celebration (timed with the spring equinox) was the most important festival and involved delegates from all over the empire presenting tributes, such as lions, bulls, and cloth, to the king. Depictions of such gift-giving are the subject of the relief sculptures of the immense Apadana (audience hall), with its 10,000 seating capacity.

Persepolis was excavated in the 1930s by French archeologist André Godard, who submitted the theory that the site was chosen by Cyrus the Great (590–530 BCE), founder of the Persian Empire, and that Darius I took up the challenge of constructing a site worthy of the glory of the empire.

...the ruins of this palace complex are some of the most awe-inspiring on the globe.

Burj Al Arab Hotel,
DUBAI

Soaring a staggering 963 ft (321 m) into the sky, the Burj Al Arab Hotel in Dubai, United Arab Emirates, revels in the title of tallest hotel in the world. Designed as a symbol of Dubai's ultramodernity, the spectacular boat-shaped hotel cost US$ 650 million to build and situate on a specially created island nearly 900 ft (300 m) from the shore of Jumeirah Beach. The hotel can be reached by the curved connecting bridge or by helicopter (a suspended helipad is located near its summit).

Architect Tom Wright set out to construct for Dubai a building to equal the iconic stature of the Eiffel Tower in Paris, France, and the Opera House in Sydney, Australia. By creating a building in the shape of a dhow (a traditional Arab sailing vessel), he has certainly created a memorable structure for modern times.

While the exterior of the hotel is ultra-modern and sculptural, the interior is a compilation of lavish and luxurious architectural styles from both the east and the west, as shown in the massive atrium (left), which takes up over one-third of the interior space.

Completed in 2000, the building is adapted to local climate conditions and includes a fiberglass fabric sail that allows a soft light into the hotel while protecting its inhabitants from the glare and heat of the sun.

As well as the tallest atrium in the world—an impressive 560 ft (180 m) high—the hotel boasts 202 bedroom suites on 28 double-story floors. Starting at a cost of US$ 1,000 per night, prices rise to US$ 28,000 for a single night in the Royal Suite. Described by one reviewer as a "theater of opulence," the hotel has quickly earned worldwide iconic status.

Golden Temple,
INDIA

The most sacred shrine for Sikhs, the magnificent gilded Harimandir Sahib ("Temple of God") in the Punjab, India, is a magnet for both spiritual devotees and tourists alike. Its spiritual significance and architectural splendor are equally enhanced by the reflection of the golden building in the lake of holy water (the Sarovar) that surrounds it.

Amritsar has been a spiritual place since ancient times, when it was simply a peaceful lake. Buddha meditated here, and 2,000 years later Guru Nanak (1469–1539), the founder of Sikhism, lived here. Over subsequent centuries Nanak's followers created a shrine and contained the lake, until the Harimandir was constructed under the leadership of Arjan, the fifth Guru (1581–1606). It has been rebuilt several times since then—the last time during the 1760s.

The temple blends Hindu and Muslim architectural styles and includes marble sculptures, gilding, and precious stones, much of which were donations from the Maharaja of the Sikh Kingdom of the Punjab, Ranjit Singh (1780–1839), in the 19th century.

The temple's sanctuary houses a book of poems, hymns, and prayers called the *Ada Grantha*: the Sikhs' holy scripture. All day chanting of hymns from the book, accompanied by stringed instruments and flutes, floats across the calm lake and enhances the spiritual nature of the location.

The Sarovar ("Pool of Nectar") provided inspiration and solace long before it was sanctified by Guru Ram Das (1534–1581) during his leadership as the fourth of the Ten Gurus of Sikhism. The famous epic verse *Ramayana* was written here by Valmiki some time between 500 and 100 BCE. Today the waters are considered to have healing powers and visitors cleanse their hands and feet at the bathing *ghat* area.

Amber Fort,
INDIA

Famed for its spectacular hall of mirrors in its residential palace, the magnificent 16th-century Amber Fort near Jaipur in Rajasthan, India, is reflected clearly in the waters of Maota Lake in front of it—an apparently robust military building hiding a sumptuous residential palace within.

Commissioned by the Maharaja of Amber, Man Singh I, in 1592 the fort was completed only during the reign of Jai Singh II, who became ruler of Amber in 1699 at the age of 11. In spite of its name and exterior presentation as a rugged military base, Amber Fort is in fact a complex of beautiful gateways, ornate gardens, and splendid pavilions, temples, and palaces.

Intricate carving, beautiful mosaics, splendid paintings, and delicate mirror work combine with red sandstone and white marble to provide a remarkably luxurious home that represents a masterpiece of Hindu and Mughal design.

The residential apartments of the Maharaja include the spectacular Seesh Mahal ("Hall of Mirrors") in which thousands of small mirrors decorate the ceiling and walls so that even a single candle or ray of light will be reflected throughout and illuminate the whole room.

Other highlights of the site include the Diwan-I-Aam, the public auditorium where the Maharaja listened to people's petitions, the Sukh Niwas, a "hall of pleasure" with its advanced air-cooling system and intricate decoration, and the *Zenana* (women's apartments) with their splendid frescoes depicting Lord Krishna around the ornate courtyard.

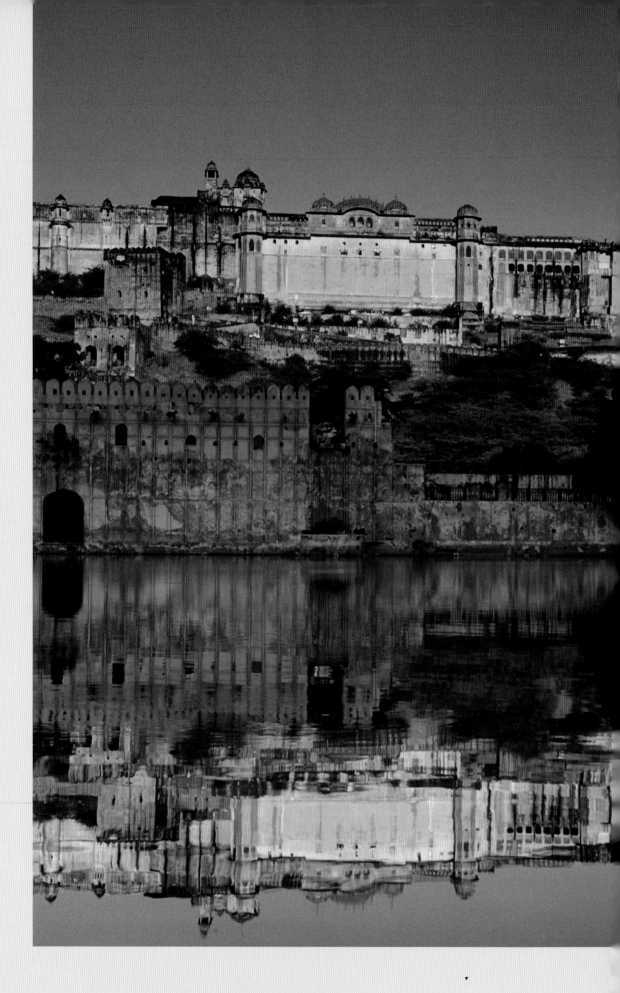

...a remarkably luxurious home that represents a masterpiece of Hindu and Mughal design.

Taj Mahal, INDIA

A quintessential symbol of India, the Taj Mahal mausoleum in Agra is a paragon of Mughal architecture as well as one of the most romantic buildings in the world, commissioned as it was by a grieving, love-sick emperor to honor his cherished wife.

In 1631 the Mughal emperor Shah Jahan lost Mumtaz Mahal, his second wife, when she gave birth to their fourteenth child. His overwhelming grief led him to have the Taj Mahal built in her name.

Requiring a total workforce of 22,000 people, the mausoleum itself was constructed between 1632 and 1648 and the gardens and other structures were completed in 1653. Harmonizing features that hallmark Persian and Indian architecture, the design is elegant and symmetrical.

The emperor refined Mughal style by using white marble inlaid with precious and semiprecious stones instead of the usual sandstone. One remarkable effect of this refinement is that the Taj Mahal takes on different hues depending on the time of day. Coupled with the elegant reflections in the pools in front of the mausoleum, at times the building itself seems magically to float above its redstone platform.

In its lavish construction, the Taj Mahal required such quantities of precious stones and white marble that the treasury was near bankrupted. As a consequence, the emperor was dethroned and imprisoned. Visible from his prison window was the Taj, the mausoleum where he would eventually join his beloved wife.

The stones that were used to build the Taj Mahal were brought from as far away as Tibet and Sri Lanka, and it took a fleet of 1,000 elephants to transport them to the site.

...at times the building itself seems magically to float above its redstone platform.

Varanasi, INDIA

At least 3,000 years old and—according to tradition—founded by the
Indian god Shiva, Varanasi on the banks of the River Ganges in the
state of Uttar Pradesh is the oldest surviving city in the world and
one of the holiest Hindu pilgrimage sites in India.

Over one million Hindu pilgrims make their way to Varanasi's magnificent holy shrines and temples to the deities Shiva and Shakti every year. Pilgrims come here to bathe in the sacred waters of the River Ganges because they believe that it will cleanse them of their sins and put an end to the cycle of rebirth.

Ritual bathing is enabled by a series of about 100 famed *ghats* (stone stairways that descend directly into the river). The most celebrated *ghat* is Dasaswamedh, which taken literally means "river front of ten sacrificed horses": the name refers to the legend that Brahma (Hinduism's creator god) made the animal sacrifice to ensure Lord Shiva's return from banishment. This *ghat*, which is often visited by *Sadhus*, or Hindu holy men, is set against a spectacular array of temples and shrines, and the bathing ritual at Dasaswamedh is one of the city's most beautiful and iconic images.

Pilgrims come here to bathe in the sacred waters
of the River Ganges...

Kathmandu Valley, NEPAL

Surveyed by the iconic Swayambhunath Stupa shrine featuring the all-seeing eyes of Buddha, the Kathmandu Valley in Nepal is home to some of the most outstanding Buddhist and Hindu temples and palaces in the world.

The valley is also the location of three cities: Patan, Bhaktapur, and Nepal's capital, Kathmandu, the last named for a distinctive temple in its main Durbar Square. The wooden two-story pagoda is called Kasthamandap Temple, which translates from the original Sanskrit as "wood-covered shelter." The pagoda is said to be built from the wood of a single tree and, remarkably, no nails or supports were used in its construction.

The most ancient of all the holy shrines is the magnificent and enigmatic Swayambhunath Stupa. It commands the hillside overlooking Kathmandu with its golden spire, huge white dome, and pair of all-seeing eyes painted on each of its four façades. The stupa (the term for a Buddhist shrine) is on a pilgrimage site that has been important to Buddhists and Hindus alike since the 5th century CE, and the temple complex is vibrant with prayer wheels, shrines, smaller temples, and Shiva *lingams*.

Patan—the most beautiful city in the Kathmandu Valley —hosts four stupas thought to have been commissioned in the 3rd century BCE by Charumati, daughter of Buddhist Indian Emperor Ashoka the Great (304–232 BCE). The majestic stupas are sited on mounds at four corners of the city, giving Patan the sense of being a monastic city.

Bhaktapur, also known as the "City of Devotees," is the most medieval of the three cities, rich in ancient art and architecture with its huge square, ornate pagodas, monasteries, palaces, and monuments, with, in the background, the towering outline of the Himalayas.

...a pilgrimage site ...important to Buddhists and Hindus alike since the 5th century CE.

Mount Everest,
THE HIMALAYAS

The crowning glory of the Himalayas on the Tibetan–Nepalese border, Mount Everest is at 29,000 ft (9,700 m) the world's highest mountain above sea level. It formed about 60 million years ago, but it was only discovered to be the earth's tallest peak by Indian surveyor Radhanath Sikdar in 1852.

The British Surveyor General of India Andrew Waugh named the mountain in 1865 after his predecessor Colonel Sir George Everest (1790–1866), who was the first westerner to record the location of the mountain. However, its Tibetan name is Chomolungma, meaning "Mother of the Universe," and the Nepalese name is Sagarmatha, meaning "Goddess of the Sky."

Former New Zealand beekeeper Sir Edmund Hillary and the Nepalese Sherpa Tenzing Norgay became the first to reach the summit in 1953. Since then, about 2,500 people have ascended to the peak, although the mountain has also claimed nearly 200 lives. With its freezing temperatures, high winds, avalanches, and icefalls, Everest is a particularly dangerous mountain to climb.

Climbers will typically spend less than a half-hour on "top of the world." They will need to descend before darkness sets in, afternoon weather becomes a serious problem, or supplemental oxygen tanks run out.

The Qinghai–Tibet Railroad, CHINA

Speeding along past yaks and antelopes into the cloud-shrouded mountains of Tibet, China's "Sky Train" journeys for two days on the Qinghai Railroad from Beijing to Lhasa on an astonishing route that earns it the title of the world's highest railroad.

A marvel of modernity, the train boasts carriages that are fitted with oxygen masks because air becomes very thin when the train reaches the mountains. The railroad peaks at a height of over 16,404 ft (5,468 m) on the Tibetan Plateau—a point at which passengers would risk altitude sickness were oxygen not pumped into the compartments.

Completing the 683 miles (1,100 km) of track and the new fleet of trains in 2006 cost the Chinese government about US\$ 4.2 billion. The hefty price is due to the fact that much of the route followed by the railroad is across mountain passes and ravines, and certain stretches are constructed on permafrost.

In some sections the track has an innovative ground cooling system that is vital to stop the tundra's permafrost melting and making the track unstable. Elsewhere the track is elevated above the ground. The resulting sight of this very costly construction provides one of the most incredible aspects of the railroad as the trains seem to float above the tundra.

More than 596 miles (960 km), or over 80 percent of this extraordinary feat of engineering, reach an altitude of more than 12,000 ft (4,000 m), and there are 675 bridges.

Potala Palace, TIBET

The Potala Palace is the most impressive structure in Tibet.
Perching on the side of Marpo Ri (Red Mountain) in Lhasa at
11,480 ft (3,800 m) above sea level, this former home of the Dalai
Lama is also the highest palace in the world.

Legend has it that Marpo Ri was the site of a sacred cave inhabited by the Bodhisattva Chenresig, the "Buddha of Compassion." His spirit is said to be reincarnated in Tibet's succession of Dalai Lamas. In the 7th century CE, Emperor Songtsen Gampo used the cave as a meditation retreat and then, in 637, he built a palace on the mountain. This was subsumed into the current palace when work was started on it in 1645 under the fifth Dalai Lama. In 1648 the lower part of the building—the Potrang Karpo ("the White Palace")—was ready for the Dalai Lama and his household to occupy as a winter palace.

The palace was used as headquarters of the local government, as well as serving as a venue for state ceremonies and as the site of a religious school for training monks. The palace also houses the tombs of former Dalai Lamas and consequently acts as a pilgrimage center. The Potala's most venerated statue is that of Arya Lokeshvara, which attracts thousands of pilgrims daily.

The upper part of the building—Potrang Marpo ("the Red Palace")—was constructed between 1690 and 1694 using over 7,000 laborers and 1,500 artists and craftsmen. In all, the palace boasts over 1,000 rooms covering more than 5 square miles (13 km²). It contains over 10,000 altars and 200,000 statues, and houses some of the finest examples of Tibetan art in the world, including detailed handiwork from the last 1,300 years featuring traditional symbols such as the dharma wheel, lotus flowers, and goldfish.

…the palace boasts over 1,000 rooms covering
more than 5 square miles (13 km²).

Shwedagon Pagoda, MYANMAR

A glittering golden feast for the eyes, the Shwedagon Pagoda is an enormous Buddhist shrine, or stupa, in Yangon, the largest city in Myanmar (formerly Burma). At a towering 300 ft (100 m) in height, it is a distinctive feature of the city skyline: the English author Somerset Maugham described it in 1930 as "rising superbly upwards like a sudden hope in the dark night of the soul."

A paragon of Burmese temple architecture, Shwedagon is considered to be one of the holiest sites in Myanmar because it contains relics of four previous Buddhas, including eight hairs from Siddhartha Gautama, the founder of Buddhism. Legend has it that while trading in India in 585 BCE Tapussa and Bhallika, two merchant brothers from Myanmar, met the historical Buddha, who presented them with the hair relics. On their return to Myanmar, the Shwedagon Pagoda was built to enshrine the relics.

Over the centuries the stupa has been updated and enhanced—notably by Queen Shinsawpu in 1451, who is responsible for having the building covered in gold, and by King Sinbyushin of Inwa in 1775, who increased the height of the structure to its current 300 ft (100 m).

The shimmering appearance of the stupa is created by over 20,000 solid gold bars and its beauty is enhanced by its adornment with a vast array of precious gems. The summit of the stupa is studded with over 5,000 diamonds and more than 2,000 rubies, sapphires, and other valuable stones. It is also decorated with over 1,000 golden bells; and at the peak is a single 76-carat diamond.

The present-day main stupa is surrounded by eight smaller stupas, as well as an array of beautifully carved and decorated shrines, statues, and elegant, lacquered pavilions, including one containing the Maha Titthaganda, a three-toned bell. Weighing in at 42 tons, it is one of the heaviest bells in the world.

...Shwedagon is considered to be one of the holiest sites in Myanmar...

Gobi Desert,
ASIA

Covering 500,000 square miles (1.3 million km²) in southern Mongolia and northern China, the Gobi is Asia's biggest desert and the fifth largest on the planet.

The Gobi Desert receives less than 8 in (20 cm) of precipitation on its north-eastern borders and is for the most part completely dry. It is composed of barren gravel plains and is subject to extremes of temperature—up to 90°F (32°C) in summer, plummeting to -40°F (-40°C) in winter—and fierce sandstorms are not unusual.

Despite the harsh climate and the fact that it is almost 3,000 ft (1,000 m) above sea level, the scrubland and grassy steppe areas provide enough grazing to support the flocks of nomadic tribes, who mostly raise goats for their cashmere wool. Water supplies are uncertain and scarce but some can be found in small lakes and wells.

The first report of a sighting of the Gobi Desert by a European was by Venetian trader and explorer Marco Polo in 1275. Exploration by US naturalist Roy Chapman Andrews early in the last century led to the discovery of fossilized dinosaur eggs belonging to the oviraptor, a birdlike omnivore standing over 6 ft (2 m) high.

Today the desert is home to an astonishing array of wildlife, particularly considering the harshness of its climate: snow leopards, gobi bears, gazelles, ibex, wild horses and asses, jerboa (rodents), wild camels, wolves, musk oxen, lizards, and golden eagles can all be found here.

Lake Baikal, RUSSIA

The deepest lake in the world, Lake Baikal in the south of Siberia, is also the biggest freshwater lake and one of the most ancient in existence. It is home to the Baikal seal (or *nerpa*) as well as 1,550 species and varieties of animal, including the famous omul fish, and over 1,000 species of aquatic flora.

The lake stretches for nearly 400 miles (636 km), averaging 16 miles (48 km) in width but reaching nearly 50 miles (80 km) in places. Its depth averages 2,190 ft (730 m) but it has a maximum point of 4,860 ft (1,620 m)— the equivalent of five Eiffel Towers. Baikal contains about one-fifth of the world's reserves of fresh water and over 80 percent of the former Soviet Union's supply. It is said that all of the world's rivers combined—including the Ganges and the Amazon— would take a year to fill the lake.

The lake's waters are home to over 100 species of molluscs, which serve as nutrition to fish such as sturgeon, sig, grayling, bullhead, eel-pout, and the omul—a salmon-like fish found only in Lake Baikal—which in its smoked form is a local delicacy. The lake is also home to the *nerpa*, freshwater seals who are believed to have arrived at the lake during prehistoric times. Their closest relatives are Arctic seals. Silver-skinned and graceful, they bask in the sun or make dens in the snow, and are an appealing feature of the lake.

Baikal also features several islands, the biggest of which is Olkhon. Over 60 miles (100 km) long, the island exhibits a diverse landscape, including taiga (coniferous forest), steppe (treeless grassland), and even a small desert. Legend has it that the "conqueror of the universe" is buried here, believed by some to be the 13th-century Mongol warrior Genghis Khan. The island also carries the title of the world's second largest lake-bound island (after Manitoulin Island on Lake Huron, USA).

Baikal contains about one-fifth of the world's reserves of fresh water...

The Great Wall of China, ASIA

It may not be visible from the moon, as popular thought would have it, but the Great Wall of China is nonetheless the earth's longest construction and an extraordinary human achievement. Crossing deserts, grasslands, mountains, and plateaus, it winds for 4,165 miles (6,700 km) from Shanhaiguan Pass in the east to Jiayuguan Pass in the west (an equivalent distance would be from New York to Los Angeles and back again).

Qin Shi Huang, the First Emperor of China during the Qin Dynasty (221–206 BCE), is believed to have initiated the building of the Great Wall after unifying the seven warring states to form China. He joined and enhanced four preexisting defence walls made from packed earth in the north of China, and stationed troops along them. The resulting wall was built further north than the current wall and in fact a little of it still exists.

The present Great Wall was mostly constructed during the Ming Dynasty (1348–1644 CE) as a means of defence against raids by Mongols and Turkic tribes. Constructed from bricks and stone after the Mongol victory at Tumu in 1449 CE, this wall was on average 16 ft (5 m) wide and 33 ft (11 m) high. It also enjoyed additional defense features, such as watchtowers, cannons, garrison posts, and beacon towers to warn of approaching enemies.

A "must-see" for every visitor to China, it can however be exhausting to traverse as the steps that form the wall are very steep in some areas. Watchtowers (left) were built on high points along the wall.

The present Great Wall was mostly constructed during the Ming Dynasty (1348–1644 CE)...

Lijiang, CHINA

Known as the "Venice of the East," Lijiang old town in Yunnan Province, China, revels in an elaborate and beautiful waterway system lined by reconstructed traditional wooden Chinese buildings. The town was created 800 hundred years ago during the late Song Dynasty and early Yuan Dynasty. Its inhabitants refer to it as Dayan, a calligrapher's ink stone, because its streets, alleyways, canals, and streams meander on the hillside like free-flowing ink on a slab.

The waterways are fed mainly from Black Dragon Pool, water from which is channeled into streams to every part of the old town, sometimes even running underneath houses. Over 350 elegant and ornate bridges (some from the Ming Dynasty) can be found crossing the town's waterways. A sluice in the town center is opened nightly to wash mud and dust from the bluestone pavements.

Once an important trading post on the Silk Road, Lijiang became a town of national importance after Kublai Khan (1215–1294) stationed troops here in 1253. Khan, a Mongol military leader destined to be the first Emperor of the Yuan Dynasty, set the town on a path to becoming the main center for politics, education, and culture in the region. Although renowned for his military might, Khan was also enamored with Chinese culture and in Lijiang he founded the first classical orchestra for the Naxi, a local ethnic group.

Temple of the Emerald Buddha, THAILAND

Sparkling spires and vibrant mosaics feature highly at the 18th-century Temple of the Emerald Buddha (Wat Phra Kae), Thailand's holiest and most significant sacred structure, which is built inside the grounds of the Royal Palace in Bangkok.

The temple is home to the Emerald Buddha, a statue made in fact of green jade and measuring about 27 in (70 cm) high. The statue—believed to date from the 15th century—has been housed at the temple since it was constructed as part of the founding of Bangkok in 1782 CE. The Thai people attribute the statue with great spiritual importance, and the king changes its attire three times a year. In the rainy season the little statue sports a golden monk's robe, in the hot season a gold and diamond robe, and in the cool season a solid gold robe.

Within its cloisters the temple also includes nearly 200 wallpaintings detailing images of the Thai interpretation of the Hindu epic the *Ramayana*, created during the reign of King Mongkut (Rama IV, 1825–1850 CE).

A particular highlight of the complex is the Royal Pantheon with its lifesize statues of the kings of the Chakri Dynasty, "guarded" by enormous mythical statues, such as the Hindu *garuda* bird and the part-bird part-woman *kinaree*.

The temple is home to the Emerald Buddha, a statue made in fact of green jade...

Petronas Twin Towers,
KUALA LUMPUR

At a breathtaking 1,356 ft (452 m) high, the Petronas Twin Towers in Kuala Lumpur, Malaysia, are the world's tallest twin towers and a triumph for American architect César Pelli.

The two towers were commissioned by Petronas, Malaysia's national oil company, with the aim of constructing the planet's highest structure. When they were completed in 1998, at a cost of US$1.2 billion, the 88-story towers were indeed the tallest buildings in the world, and remained so until the 101-story, 1,527-ft (509-m) high Taipei 101 grabbed the title for China in 2003.

The floor plate design of the towers is based on geometric principles of Islamic architecture, a reflection of the architect's desire to combine tradition with modernity. A 180-ft (60-m) skybridge joining the two towers at their 41st and 42nd floors allows access from one building to another at a point where there is a viewing podium accessible to the public.

Visible from anywhere in the city, the twin towers are constructed largely of reinforced concrete, with a steel and glass façade designed to resemble motifs found in Islamic art.

Petronas occupies one of the towers; the other is mostly let to multinational companies. Both rise up against the attractive setting of Kuala Lumpur City Center park, to form an unequaled feature of the Kuala Lumpur skyline

The floor plate design of the towers is based on geometric principles of Islamic architecture...

Angkor Wat, CAMBODIA

Featuring on Cambodia's national flag, the 12th-century temple of Angkor Wat is the country's top tourist attraction and one of the world's grandest buildings. Overgrown by jungle for centuries, the "lost city" of Angkor was rediscovered and its splendor revealed to the world by French explorer Henri Mahout in 1860.

Suryavarman II, King of the Khmer Empire (1113–1150 CE) ordered the site at Angkor to be developed as his main city and principal temple. The temple was originally designed for the worship of the Hindu god Vishnu but was converted to a Theravada Buddhist temple in the 14th or 15th century (and it remains so today).

The Angkor Wat (meaning "City Temple") is a true masterpiece of classical Khmer architecture. It blends two traditional Khmer temple designs, namely the temple mountain and the galleried temple. Temple mountain designs symbolized Mount Meru (where Hindu gods lived), and galleried temples featured open or half-open passageways. The Wat includes towers shaped like lotus buds and is decorated with bas-reliefs (painting-like sculptures) that feature *devatas*, or heavenly nymphs. Stories from Hindu

The majestic Angkor Wat is often praised for the harmony of its design, which has been compared to the architecture of ancient Greece or Rome.

mythology are depicted on the bas-relief on the temple's outer gallery—believed to be the longest unbroken bas-relief known in existence.

Surrounded by a moat and a wall almost 2.5 miles (4 km) long, the temple area covers more than 980,000 square yards (820,000 m²). Angkor Wat is a magnificient testament to the former glory of the Khmer capital.

Krakatau Island,
INDONESIA

Famous for producing the biggest bang and one of the most devastating eruptions in human history, the Krakatau volcano is part of an archipelago in the middle of the Sunda Strait between Sumatra and Java in Indonesia.

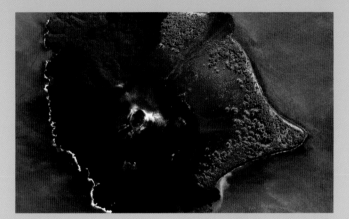

Anak Krakatau is still active. Since the 1950s, the island has grown at an average rate of 5 inches (13 cm) per week.

The original Krakatau volcano is estimated to have been over 6,000 ft (2,000 m) high but in 416 CE a violent eruption reduced it to about a quarter of this height and created three islands: Rakata, Sertung, and Panjang.

Of the volcano's many eruptions, however, the most celebrated occurred in 1883, when shock waves were felt worldwide for several days afterward and explosions were heard over 3,000 miles (nearly 5,000 km) away in Mauritius.

Estimated to be 20,000 times more powerful than an atomic bomb, the eruption produced a 120-ft (40-m) high tsunami that killed over 36,000 people and damaged or destroyed 300 towns and villages in Java and Sumatra. It also produced about 6 cubic miles (25 km³) of volcanic debris that covered an area of almost 200 square miles (500 km²) and seemed to eclipse the sun.

A new volcano, Anak Krakatau (meaning "child of Krakatau"), appeared in 1927, 44 years after the major eruption. Today, at 656 ft (211 m) above sea level and over a mile (2 km) in diameter, the volcano is continuing to grow.

Qin Terracotta Warriors, CHINA

Discovered by farmers drilling for a well in 1974, the Terracotta Warriors are a collection of over 8,000 life-size figures that had been buried over 2,000 years ago with the First Emperor of Qin near Xi'an in Shaanxi Province, one of the Four Great Ancient Capitals of China.

Destined to become the First Emperor of all China, Qin Shi Huang came to power in 246 BCE at the age of 13 and almost immediately commissioned work on the figures of the Imperial Guard for his mausoleum, which took perhaps as many as 700,000 workers 11 years to complete.

It is believed the figures—of various ranks of soldiers and their horses–were produced in a style equivalent to today's mass production, because each is constructed from a range of parts that were assembled after firing rather than being formed from a single piece of terracotta. However, the striking feature of the warriors is that each has an individual lifelike face—the work of craftsmen.

Remarkably, each warrior's face was carved individually and no two faces are the same.

Originally the funerary figures had real armor and weapons (subsequently stolen) and they were positioned in battle formation according to rank. The aim of burying them with the Emperor was to help him to wage war and become the dominant force in the afterlife.

Borobudur, INDONESIA

Created in the 8th century and subsequently covered by volcanic ash and overgrown with jungle, the Buddhist stupa of Borobudur in Java, Indonesia, is a true lost treasure. Rediscovered in 1814, it has been completely restored and now ranks as the world's largest Buddhist shrine, and one of the most popular Buddhist pilgrimage (and tourist) sites on the planet.

Little is known of the origins of the stupa or, indeed, its subsequent abandonment. The most convincing theory is that it was deserted because of the country's conversion to Islam in the 15th century. What is certain, however, is that it was rediscovered thanks largely to Sir Thomas Stamford Raffles (1781–1826), Governor-General of Java under British administration (1811–1816).

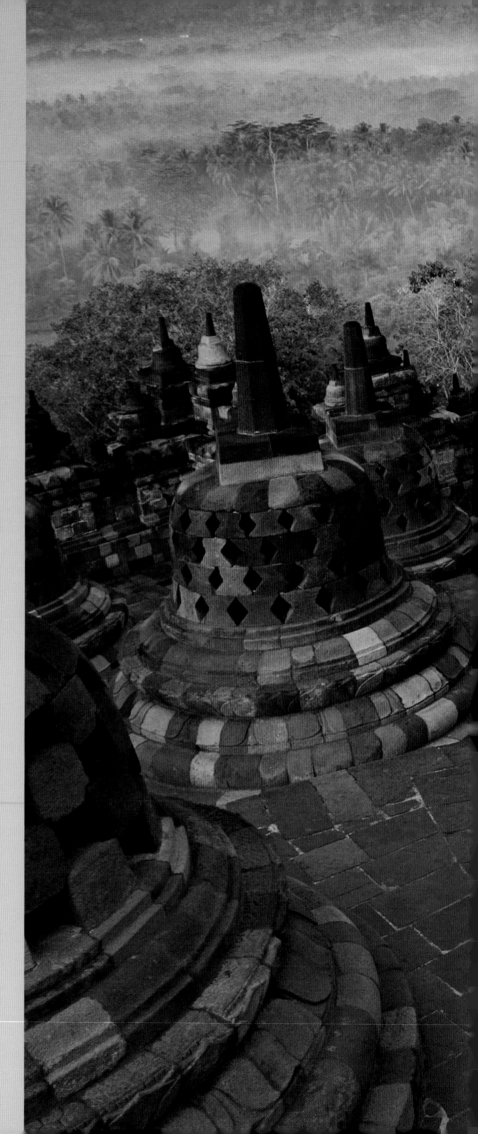

The temple of Borobudur is surrounded by an idyllic landscape of rice-terraced hills and overlooked by four volcanoes. Crowning the entire structure is a great central stupa, which represents Nirvana.

The stupa rediscovered by Raffles' team in 1814 comprises nine platforms—six square, three round—placed on top of each other to create a mandala (an important Buddhist symbol of the universe used in meditation). The platforms, the largest of which is almost 1,300 ft^2 (120 m^2), are adorned with nearly 3,000 beautifully carved relief panels that depict scenes from Buddha's life or Buddhist stories and over 500 Buddha statues. The upper platforms feature a large stupa surrounded by 72 small perforated stupas in the shape of a bell.

Pilgrims climb to the large stupa at the top of the temple by a set anticlockwise route of stairways and corridors through the series of platforms. Each platform represents a stage of enlightenment; at the top of the structure pilgrims symbolically reach Nirvana (the end of suffering).

Zhangjiajie National Forest Park, CHINA

Famed for its unusually shaped quartzite sandstone pillars soaring into misty clouds, the Zhangjiajie National Forest Park is the first of its kind in China and one of the most popular tourist attractions in the country.

Established in 1982, the park's lush subtropical forest covers an area of about 185 square miles (480 km²) and is home to a huge range of animals, including protected species such as the Golden Pheasant, the Musk Deer, the Giant Salamander, and the Rhesus Monkey.

A highlight of the park is the Yellow Stone Stronghold (Huangshizhai). At almost 4,000 ft (1,330 m) above sea level, the structure offers one of the park's best observation points from which to view the splendidly named peaks: Six Wonders Pavilion, Five Fingers Peaks, Clouds Drifting Cave, and Golden Turtle in the Clouds Sea. The peaks have inspired Chinese artists and are a familiar symbol of Chinese landscape imagery.

The park also includes Golden Whip Stream, a 4.6-mile (7.5-km) long waterway deemed by many to be one of the most beautiful in the world. Surrounded by steep cliffs and verdant forest, its clear water teeming with colorful fish, the stream appears to flow through a fairytale landscape.

The peaks have inspired Chinese artists and are a familiar symbol of Chinese landscape imagery.

Hong Kong's Harbor & Cityscape, CHINA

Embracing some of the tallest skyscrapers ever built, the skyline along Hong Kong's Victoria Harbor is ranked as the most visually impressive in the world. The harbor itself, which divides Hong Kong Island from the Kowloon Peninsula, is up to 45 ft (15 m) deep in places.

Hong Kong was a small outpost when it was seized by the British during the First Opium War with China (1839–1842), primarily because of its large and sheltered harbor. Today it is home to four of the highest skyscrapers on earth: Two International Finance Center (1,245 ft/415 m), Central Plaza (1,122 ft/374 m), Bank of China Tower (1,101 ft/367 m), and the Center (1,038 ft/346 m). Skyscraper height restrictions were lifted in Kowloon following the closure of a nearby airport and work is underway on even taller buildings, including the International Commerce Center, destined to be Hong Kong's tallest building (and the fourth tallest in the world) when finished in 2010.

Continuing land reclamation projects mean that further skyscrapers are inevitable, but they come at the cost of a reduced harbor size. Nonetheless, the harbor remains one of the busiest in the world: about 220,000 oceangoing and river vessels use its port facilities every year.

The iconic Star Ferry service, operating between Kowloon and Hong Kong Island since 1888, offers passengers a spectacular panoramic view of the harbor and skyline.

Container vessels, junks, sampans, and pleasure craft glide around Hong Kong's Victoria Harbor, famous for its backdrop of the city's panoramic view and skyline.

...the harbor is one of the busiest in the world...

Forbidden City,
CHINA

The residence of 24 past emperors of the Ming and Qing dynasties between 1420 and 1911 CE, China's Forbidden City in Beijing is the largest palace complex in the world.

Tradition has it that the Forbidden City is named for the fact that at one time those entering it without royal permission would be put to death. Today, the Chinese government have officially renamed the site GuGong (meaning "Old Palace" or "Palace Museum").

The complex was commissioned in 1406 CE by the third Ming Emperor, Yong Le, when he moved the capital of China to Beijing from Nanjing. Measuring 2,460 by 3,150 ft (820 by 1,050 m), the Forbidden City is enclosed by a 30-ft (10-m) high wall that is surrounded by a 20-ft (7-m) deep moat. The structure contains about 1,000 rooms designed to accommodate its 6,000 inhabitants at the height of its fame, including the emperor, his court, and their servants.

A highlight of the complex is the Hall of Supreme Harmony. The largest wooden structure in China and a symbol of imperial power, it was also the tallest structure of its day—in fact, at the time of its construction it was forbidden to build any edifice higher than it.

The hall is built on a three-tier marble terrace, contains 72 pillars, and measures 115 ft (38 m) high, 210 ft (70 m) wide, and over 120 ft (40 m) long. It is richly decorated with gold lacquer and images of dragons, and within it are significant objects and works of art, including bronze *dings* (ancient Chinese vessels), bronze cranes and tortoises, a sundial, and huge bronze vats.

Banaue Rice Terraces,
PHILIPPINES

Hewn by hand from the Ifugao Mountains in the Philippines over 2,000 years ago, the Banaue Rice Terraces range over 3,860 square miles (1,000 km²) and show the ingenuity and assiduity of humankind.

The Banaue Rice Terraces—a Unesco World Heritage Site—are wondrous vertical gardens, sculpted from the earth by hand.

Designed to be irrigated by channels formed from the streams and springs that issue from the rainforests above them, the Banaue terraces were developed in order to grow rice and vegetables. The terraces, shaped like an amphitheater, start at the base of the mountains and rise up to almost 3,000 ft (1,000 m) above sea level. They represent a remarkable engineering achievement, are thought to have been created with minimal equipment and largely by hand, and would allegedly encircle half the globe if laid end to end.

Ifugao means "people of the earth" and refers both to the province in which the terraces are located and the indigenous people who helped to create them. The Ifugao people's development of the rice terraces to help supply a sustainable source of food showed an astounding appreciation of watershed management. To this day, the Ifugao continue traditional farming methods and resist cultural assimilation. In addition, they applied engineering skills second to none in their construction of highly sophisticated and sturdy huts.

Uluru/Ayers Rock,
AUSTRALIA

Uluru/Ayers Rock is Australia's most iconic natural landmark. It is a massive mound of sandstone full of minerals that reflect the sun's light in an unusual way. The result is that the rock affords the spectator a magical, ever-changing rainbow of color that may seem to glow; it can appear crimson, blue, violet, red, orange, or yellow, depending on the time of day.

Located in Uluru-Kata Tjuta National Park in the Northern Territory, Uluru is 1,044 ft (348 m) high and over 6 miles (10 km) around the base. It ranges almost 2 miles (3 km) from east to west and about 1.2 miles (2 km) from north to south, covering an area the size of 40 football pitches. It is often compared to an iceberg because most of its bulk is below the surface: underground it reaches a depth of 3.7 miles (almost 6 km).

The rock was officially named in 1873 for the Premier of South Australia, Sir Henry Ayers (1821–1897). However, in 1985 ownership of the rock was returned to the Aborigines for whom the rock has major importance as a sacred site, and subsequently it has officially been given the dual name Uluru (its Aboriginal name)/Ayers Rock.

The Anunga Aborigines view the rock as a symbol of creation and it plays a vital role in their Dreamtime (their explanation of the origins and culture of the land and its people). Some of their stories concern the creation of the rock by their ancestral beings.

Caves found at the bottom of the rock are home to sacred paintings depicting people and objects, such as boomerangs, as well as abstract images. These paintings are added to and refined constantly by the modern Aborigines, and in this sense the rock is a living monument to Aboriginal culture.

Akashi-Kaikyo Bridge, JAPAN

A monument to modern engineering prowess, the Akashi–Kaikyo Bridge joins Kobe on Japan's main Honshu Island with Awaji Island and, with a central span stretching over 6,000 ft (2,000 m), enjoys the title of the world's longest suspension bridge.

Japan's structure took the title of longest suspension bridge from the Great Belt (StoreBaelt) bridge between the islands of Sprogø and Zealand in Denmark, which has a central span of about 5,000 ft (1,700 m) and was completed shortly before the Akashi–Kaikyo bridge in 1998. Also known as Pearl Bridge, the Akashi–Kaikyo suspension bridge took two million workers ten years to build and cost US$ 3.6 billion. The construction of the bridge had to take into account that the Akashi Strait, one of the world's busiest shipping lanes, is over 300 ft (100 m) deep; a rapid tidal current; and the need to withstand earthquakes up to 8.5 on the Richter scale and typhoon winds up to 180 miles (290 km) per hour. In 1995, the bridge survived the Kobe earthquake, which measured 7.3 on the Richter scale, although the bridge's central span was expanded by about 3 ft (1 m) as a result.

The largest support towers are 900 ft (300 m) above sea level, and the bridge can expand over 6 ft (2 m) in one day.

Temple of the Golden Pavilion, JAPAN

Casting a shimmering, glowing reflection on the aptly named Mirror Pond alongside it, the Golden Pavilion (Kinkaku-ji) in Kyoto, Japan, presents an almost otherworldly vision. The reason is that this beautifully constructed former Zen temple is covered in gold leaf, which makes it shine and glitter in the sunlight.

Originally conceived of as a residence for the retired *shogun* (military ruler) Ashikaga Yoshimitsu, the building was commissioned in 1397 CE, at a time when Kyoto was Japan's prosperous capital city. After the *shogun*'s death in 1408 his son converted the building into a Zen temple, and today it is dedicated to Kannon, the Buddhist Goddess of Mercy.

The temple was twice destroyed in civil wars in 1467 and 1567, and then in 1950 it was deliberately burnt down by a disturbed student monk from Otani University, who believed its beauty interfered too much with contemplation.

The current temple, completed in 1955, is almost completely covered in a much thicker layer of gold leaf than the previous versions. The appellation Golden Pavilion is richly deserved, although its official name is Deer Park Temple (Rokuon-ji), which relates to the Buddhist name of the *shogun* who first commissioned it.

After the *shogun*'s death in 1408 his son converted the building into a Zen temple...

Mount Fuji, JAPAN

At about 12,000 ft (4,000m) high, Mount Fuji is the highest mountain in Japan, although it ranks only 64th in the world. Known as Fuji-san in Japan, it is situated in the Fuji-Hakone-Izu National Park west of Tokyo, and on a fine day this inspiring icon can be seen from the capital.

The mountain is in fact a dormant volcano. The last eruption occurred in 1707 and was called the great Hoei eruption because it took place in the fourth year of the Hoei era. It happened seven weeks after the Hoei earthquake, one of the largest Japan has ever experienced.

Fuji-san has a special place in the hearts and minds of the Japanese people—some of whom consider it to be sacred—as well as acting as an internationally recognized symbol of Japan. It attracts about 200,000 people every year during the climbing season. The summit has been considered by many Japanese to be a spiritual site since ancient times, and it is traditional to make the ascent during the night to time arrival at the summit with the rising sun.

The mountain has inspired the work of many Japanese and international writers and artists, particularly the painter Hokusai. His *36 Views of Mount Fuji*, in the traditional *Ukiyo-e* (woodblock prints) style, have been considered outstanding works of art since their creation in 1831.

Surrounded by five lakes, clouds and poor visibility often block the view of Mount Fuji. It is best viewed in winter or early morning when the air is clear.

The mountain has inspired many Japanese and international writers and artists...

The Great Barrier Reef, AUSTRALIA

The world's biggest and most beautiful coral site, the Great Barrier Reef off the coast of Queensland, Australia, ranges over an area of 115,840 square miles (300,000 km²), roughly the size of Poland—in fact, it is so vast it can be seen from space.

The Reef system comprises over 3,000 individual coral reefs and more than 600 islands, and is considered to be about 20,000 years old. Its sealife is second to none and includes green turtles and dugong (large, gray mammals with tails resembling spades), dolphins, and whales, 1,500 species of fish (among them the Parrotfish, Butterfly fish, and Damselfish), 4,000 species of molluscs, including the cartoon-like Giant Clams, which can measure up to 5 ft (1.5 m) across and weigh nearly 440 lb (200 kg), and over 200 different types of bird, among which are the rare Herald Petrel and the Yellow Chat.

Today the Great Barrier Reef receives about two million visitors every year. The Great Barrier Marine Park Authority has been set up to minimize the damage from tourism and other potentially hazardous activities, and to promote conservation of the site. The reef also faces threats from pollution, global warming—which is thought to cause "bleaching," sometimes a coral killer—shipping accidents and attacks by Crown-of-Thorns starfish, a coral predator.

The expansive reef is visible from the Earth's orbit and is home to a wide diversity of life. It was selected as a World Heritage Site in 1981.

Sydney Opera House,
AUSTRALIA

A modern marvel, the Sydney Opera House is one of the architectural icons of the twentieth century and Australia's most internationally recognized public building. A functioning performing arts venue, it is also the headquarters of the Sydney Symphony Orchestra, the Sydney Theatre Company, and Opera Australia.

The structure was designed in 1957 by Danish architect Jørn Utzon in response to an international competition to create a performing arts venue for Sydney instigated by New South Wales Premier Joseph Cahill.

Work began in 1959, but the building was not opened by Queen Elizabeth II until 1973, owing to a catalog of mishaps and delays, including the rebuilding of the podium columns and major changes to the interior design and functions, not to mention Utzon's resignation from the project in 1966. The total cost was Aus$102 million—a far cry from its original estimated cost of $7 million.

The final result—an imposing 1,000-room structure, which measures 607 by 394 ft (202 by 131 m)—is perhaps most famous for its sail-like roof. The roof is composed of nearly 3,000 concrete sections weighing up to 15 tons and is covered with one million tiles. It is one of the world's most photographed buildings.

Situated on Bennelong Point in Sydney Harbor, the opera house is an expressionist modern design, with a series of large precast concrete "shells" forming the roofs of the structure.

Milford Sound,
NEW ZEALAND

Visited by dolphins and seals, Milford Sound on New Zealand's South Island is a spectacular 10-mile (16-km) long fjord that boasts some of the highest waterfalls and the highest sea cliff on the planet.

The fjord is known as Piopiotahi ("a single thrush") in Maori, because legend has it that a single thrush flew here to mourn the death of its partner when Hine-nui-te-Po (goddess of death) won the gift of immortality from the demigod Maui.

In 1823 sealer John Grono became the first European to visit the fjord. He called it Milford Haven after the town where he was born in Wales, UK. The first settler was Donald Sutherland in 1877, who built a hotel there. Nearby, three years later, he found the world's fifth-highest waterfalls that now bear his name: water plunges over the Sutherland Falls for 1,800 ft (600 m) in three leaps.

Milford Sound today boasts many temporary and permanent waterfalls, thanks primarily to the location being one of the wettest places in the world: it can receive anything up to 10 in (25 cm) of rain in a day. Some waterfalls, such as the Bowen Falls, are spectacular, and cascades can drop about 3,000 ft (1,000 m).

At 5,550 ft (1,850 m), the Mitre Peak is the world's highest sea cliff and forms part of the steep mountain range surrounding the fjord. The mountains are so steep that sometimes a build-up of rainwater can lead to the verdant rainforest trees losing their grip on the land, resulting in tree avalanches.

Antarctica

The icescapes of Antarctica range over an area of 5.4 million square miles (14 million km²) around the South Pole. At twice the size of Australia, Antarctica is the fifth largest continent and is classed as the world's largest desert, strange as it may sound. (Its desert classification is to do with the lack of precipitation experienced in the region.)

Antarctica is generally the coldest place on the planet. Temperatures there range between 60°F and -112°F (15°C and -80°C), and it is the site of the lowest ever recorded temperature (a frostbite-inspiring -128°F [-89°C] in 1983 at the Russian research station in Vostok).

With approximately 90 percent of the world's ice (about 98 percent of the continent is covered by ice), Antarctica has never had an indigenous population, and there are no permanent human residents.

Wildlife in Antarctica includes Snow Petrel, albatrosses, penguins (seven species including Rockhopper and Emperor), shrimp-like krill, seals, squid, icefish, and blue whales. Sadly, hunting has decimated the number of seals and whales. Elephant and fur seals are slowly increasing in numbers after near extinction in the 1800s. However, blue whales are making a much slower recovery. There are estimated to be about 1,500 blue whales today after centuries of slaughter (over 30,000 were killed in the 1920s).

British explorer James Cook (1728–1779) is thought to be the first westerner to have crossed the Antarctic Circle in 1773, but his ship was unable to get close enough to discover the continent of Antarctica. The first successful expedition to reach the South Pole was led by Norwegian adventurer Roald Amundson in 1911.

Today, Antarctica receives about 25,000 visitors annually, and between 1,000 and 4,000 people work in its research stations during the course of the year.

Picture Credits